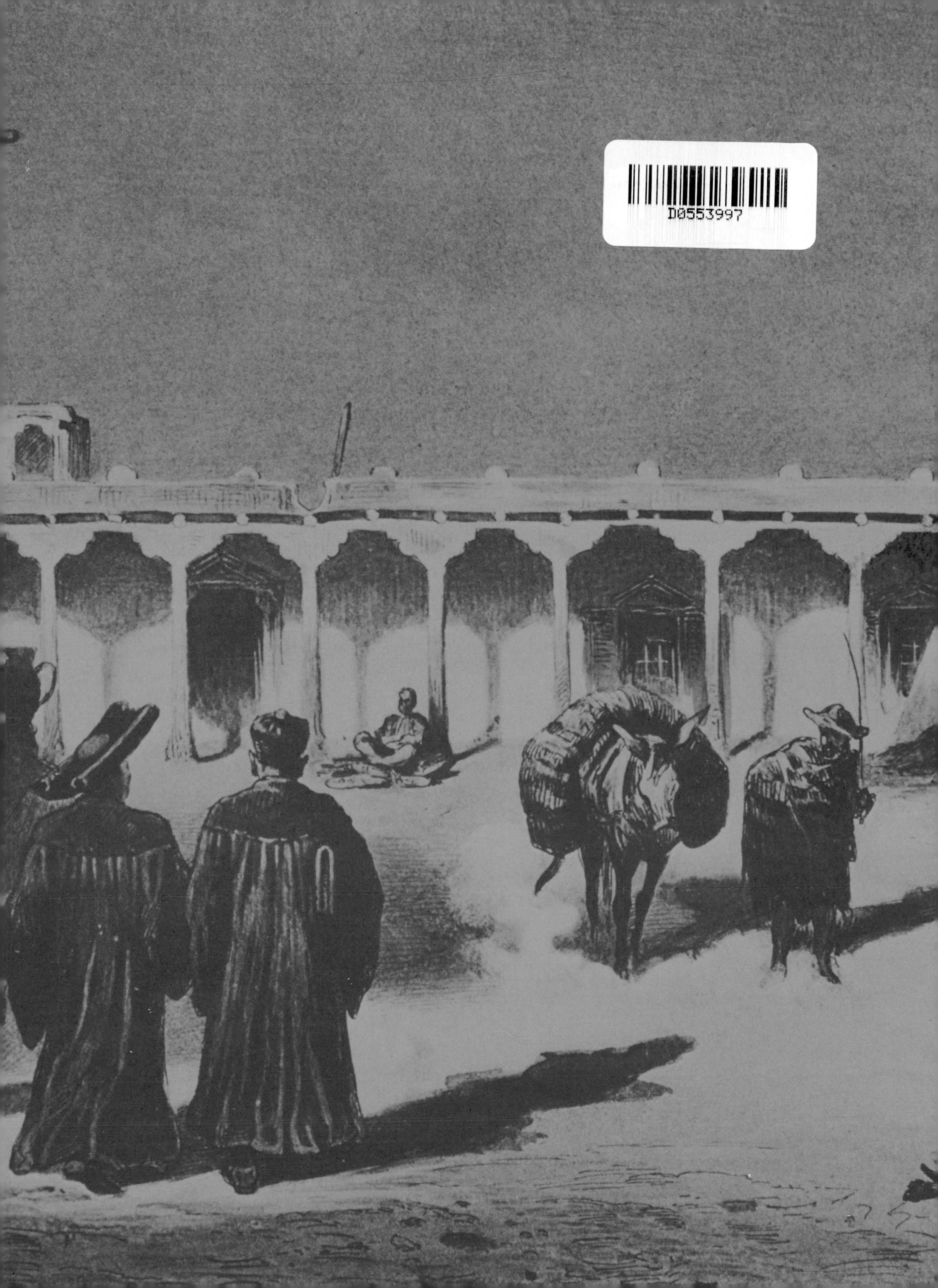

NEW MEXICO

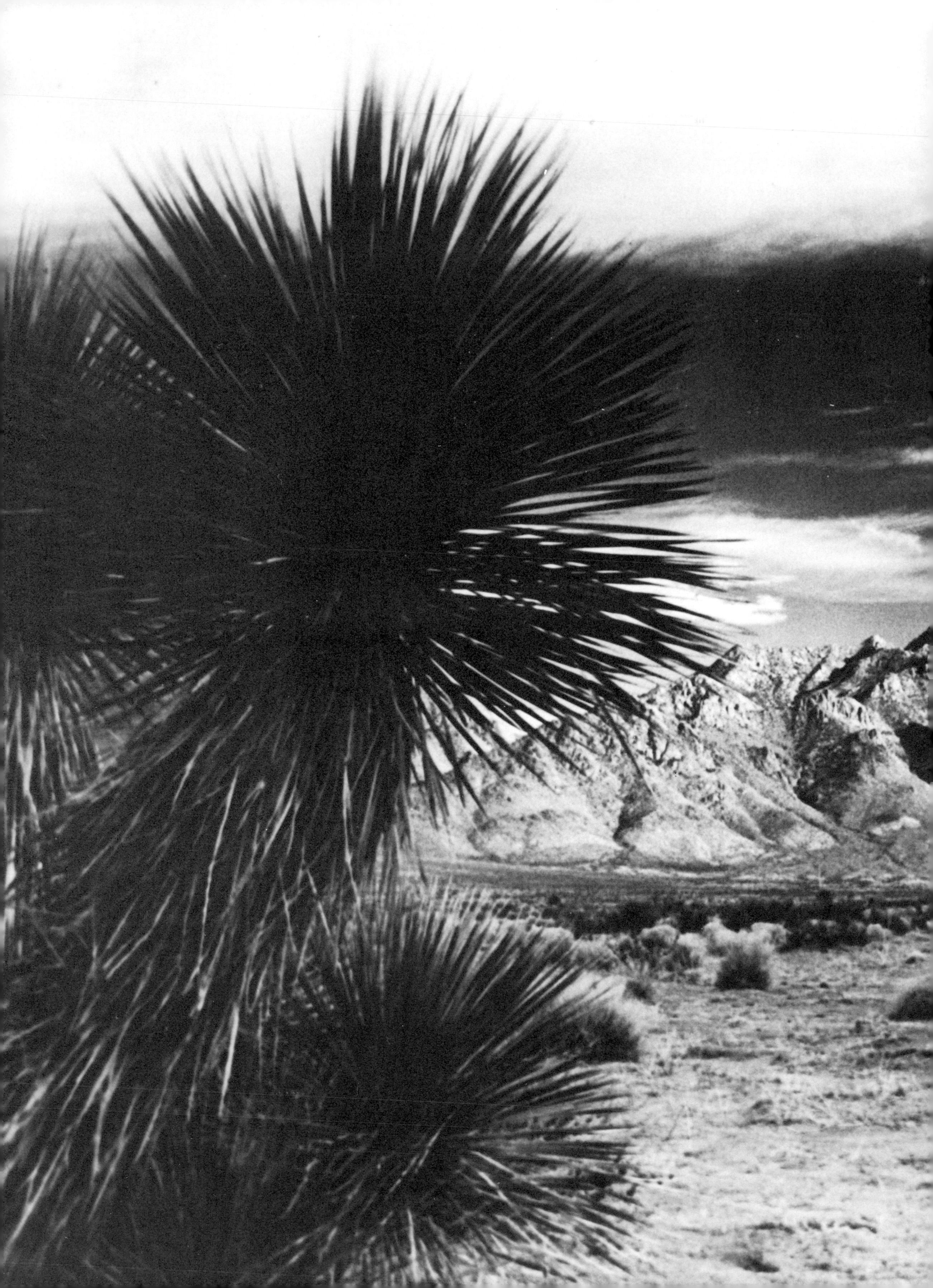

NEW MEXICO

THE DISTANT LAND

An Illustrated History by
Dan Murphy

Picture Research and
"Partners in Progress" by
John O. Baxter

Produced in cooperation with the
Historical Society of New Mexico

Windsor Publications, Inc.
Northridge, California

Windsor Publications, Inc.
History Book Division

Publisher: John M. Phillips
Editorial Director: Teri Davis Greenberg
Design Director: Alexander D'Anca

Staff for *New Mexico: The Distant Land*
Senior Editor: Laurel H. Paley
Picture Editor: Michelle Hudun
Editorial Development: F. Jill Charboneau, Leslie King, Margaret Tropp
Director, Corporate Biographies: Karen Story
Assistant Director, Corporate Biographies: Phyllis Gray
Editor, Corporate Biographies: Judith Hunter
Editorial Assistants: Kathy M. Brown, Patricia Cobb, Jerry Mosher, Lonnie Pham, Pat Pittman, Deena Tucker
Designer: J.R. Vasquez
Layout Artist: Karen McBride

Published in 1985
Printed in the United States of America
First Edition

Library of Congress Cataloging in Publication Data

Murphy, Dan.
New Mexico, the distant land.

"Produced in cooperation with the Historical Society of New Mexico."
Bibliography: p. 179
Includes index.
1. New Mexico—History. 2. New Mexico—Description and travel. 3. New Mexico—Industries. I. Historical Society of New Mexico. II. Title.
F796.M87 1985 978.9 85-9356
ISBN 0-89781-119-4

Endpapers
Pictured is a detail from German artist D.L. Cronau's 1885 work Eine Strasse in Alt-Albuquerque./Neu Mexiko. *(Please see page 122 to view this illustration in full color.) Courtesy, Amon Carter Museum, Fort Worth*

Pages 2 and 3
East of Las Cruces, the rocky Organ Mountains tower above the Southern New Mexico desert. The narrow-leafed yucca pictured on the left is one of the specialized plants able to withstand the desert's arid environment. Courtesy, New Mexico State Records Center & Archives

Pages 6 and 7
Arthur Rothstein took this photo of a Taos pueblo in New Mexico in 1936. It is from The Depression Years as Photographed by Arthur Rothstein. *Courtesy, Dover Publications*

For my
mom and dad,
who
first taught me
to love
this country

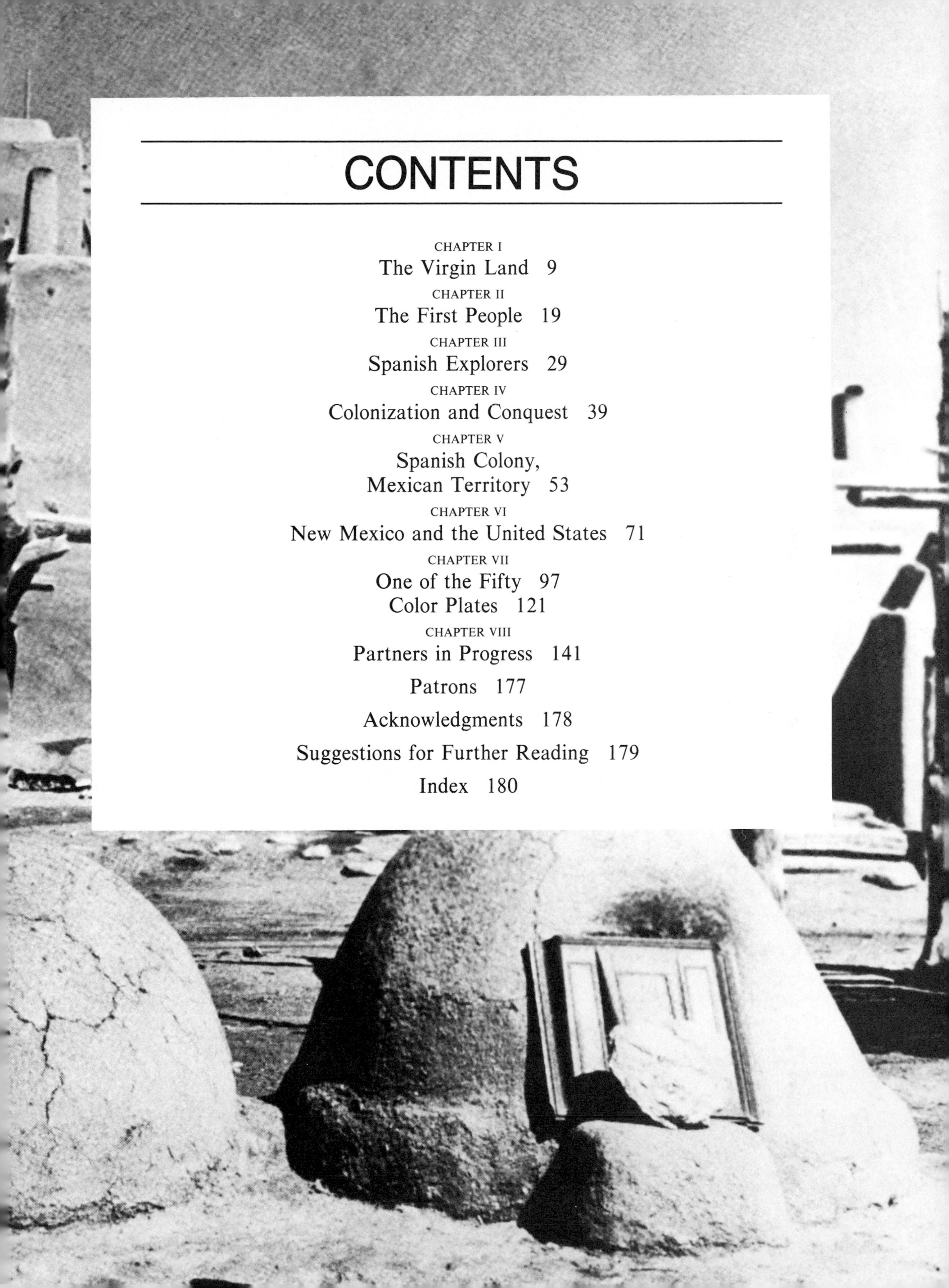

CONTENTS

Beneath a stormy sky, sheep graze in the shadow of Enchanted Mesa, near Acoma. Found throughout the state, the flat-topped hills known as mesas *are New Mexico's most distinctive geographic feature. From the Department of Development Collection, New Mexico State Records Center & Archives (NMSRCA)*

The Virgin Land

New Mexico is made out of rocks. Most states, of course, have a basement of rocks, but they are camouflaged, and the state calendars have scenes of rolling green. But in New Mexico the rocks are out in the open, great shelves and cliffs that stand baking in the sun.

New Mexico is a high land. Perhaps fifty million years ago those rocks, some of them formed beneath great seas, were slowly lifted high into the air, some warped and twisted in the process, forming spectacular mountain ranges. But the plains were lifted, too. If the governor of New Mexico, sitting in his office at Santa Fe, decided that he should sit at the same altitude as the governor of Missouri, he would have to dig a well straight down about 6,000 feet. It is the altitude that accounts for New Mexico's cold winters, unexpected in a state so far south, and the cool evenings year-round.

If the governor did decide to dig that hole beneath his office, his constituents would find it a perfectly reasonable act, providing he told them he was looking for water. New Mexico is dry. Westerly winds bring moisture from the Pacific, and the high north-central mountains often receive heavy snowfall, much to the relief of farmers and ranchers in the flatlands below who depend on snowmelt to water their crops. But in coming from the Pacific, those winds have crossed hundreds of miles and several mountain ranges, and the lion's share of water has been wrung out of them. More important to New Mexico are the springtime south and southeasterly winds that come from the Gulf of Mexico, watering the low-lying plains in the southeastern part of the state. The central spine of mountains confines most of the springtime moisture to the eastern plains, but by July moisture from the west begins to reach the Rio Grande Valley. ("It always rains on the Fourth of July picnic," say the old bean farmers in the central part of the state.) Then mornings in Santa Fe, Albuquerque, and Socorro are clear and blue, but by afternoon thunderclouds begin to form over the mountain ranges. They can be huge; the mass of a mountain range, such as the Sangre de Cristos, is enormous, yet the clouds that form on most afternoons in August are higher and wider than the range itself. The clouds promise rain and sometimes they deliver, but these are not the county-wide rains of the Midwest. Individual thunderheads move across the countryside, sometimes four or five in view at once. Some have curtains of rain hanging down that seem to disappear before reaching the ground. The appearance is correct. That is "virga," the condition when rain falls but actually evaporates before it can touch the earth. Other clouds may be dragging an actual rainstorm that will water the earth beneath it, but between such storms there may well be large areas of sunshine. One ranch can be watered while its neighbor stays dry. The state as a whole runs a moisture deficit, the amount of water evaporated in a year being greater than the amount that actually falls. In some parts of the state, particularly in the south, it would take five times as much water as is available in a normal year just to break even with what evaporates.

New Mexico is a huge state, fifth largest in the union. It is far removed from major population centers—an important factor in its history—and distances within

C H A P T E R I

Located west of the Rio Grande, between Albuquerque and Socorro, the Ladrón Mountains are a small, compact range that rise to an elevation of more than 9,000 feet. Spaniards named them "ladrón" (thief) because of the marauding bands of Navajos and Apaches that sought refuge there. NMSRCA

Beginning in Colorado as a mountain stream, the Rio Grande flows south through New Mexico's midsection and crosses the Texas border at Anthony. For centuries its turbulent waters have irrigated the crops of Indians, Hispanos, and Anglos. Early colonists called it the Rio del Norte. Courtesy, National Park Service (NPS)

the state are vast. Ranchers go a long way to town to shop, and children have long rides in school buses. With so much road per person, no state could afford a comprehensive paved highway system, and New Mexico has thousands of miles of dirt roads, much of it state highway. In Santa Fe, the capital, many of the finest homes are on dirt roads, and at the opera one may see elegantly dressed people climbing out of four-wheel-drive vehicles.

The highest part of the state is the north-central mountain core, where the Rockies come down from Colorado and extend for a hundred miles into New Mexico, finally petering out in small rounded hills and the sharp cut of Glorieta Pass. Entrepreneurs have built ski lodges up there, and there is an elk hunting season. The high country could easily be mistaken for land far to the north, with huge forests of ponderosa pine, and even Douglas fir. Hiking to the high country from one of the National Forest Service trailheads, the hiker passes through climates as though he were traveling north; every 1,000 feet upward represents perhaps 200 miles north. The hike may start in piñon-juniper scrublands, but these give way to the ponderosa, and then aspens, breathtaking in autumn. And often at their highest point the mountains seem like arctic tundra, where no trees grow but there is just rock, and miniature plants in a fierce struggle with the cold and wind, and views that go forever.

But New Mexico has another kind of mountain: the small, clearly defined range. Small is a relative term; a rancher who lives near one of these ranges may spend a lifetime learning it well. But a visitor traveling by car can see a range in its entirety, approach it, and drive past it in a few hours. Each of these ranges represents a distinct geologic event, and, especially from an airplane, they are textbook examples of the various ways mountains come to be. Mount Taylor and the Jemez range are both volcanoes. The Sandias are the product of a fault-block thrust: the west side, the side pushed up along the fault, is so steep that it supports a two-

Made of weathered sandstone, Camel Rock is a good example of what erosion has done to New Mexico's terrain. Situated north of Santa Fe near the pueblo of Tesuque, the formation has become a popular stopping place for travelers. NMSRCA

Above
During the centuries since the Jemez eruptions, the soft volcanic ash spewed forth has eroded into a series of fascinating formations. Known as "tent rocks," they continue to intrigue geologists and tourists alike. From the Woodward Collection, NMSRCA

Right
The cholla cactus, a hardy desert plant, is found in many parts of the state. When moisture is adequate, it produces a brilliant magenta blossom. NPS

mile cable tramway with a rise of almost 4,000 feet, while skiers glide down the gently sloped eastern side. These and perhaps three dozen other ranges are oases in the desert, "islands in the sky." Other geologic showplaces are the mountain canyons. Canyons are watercourses, success stories in the ages-long effort of water to claw the mountains down. Distinctive of desert mountains are the outwash plains, broad slopes that come from the canyon mouths, the temporary resting place of all the debris that came out of those canyons: the very stuff of the mountains, spread out on the desert around the base of the mountain like the skirt of a lady sitting on the grass. Early travelers knew that the mountains were sources of water. In danger of death on the desert, they headed for the outwash plains to find a major arroyo, then followed it up to where the water had not yet sunk into the debris.

Much of New Mexico is desert. Scientists define "desert" in various ways, as an area where evaporation exceeds precipitation, or where the annual rainfall is less than twenty inches. To plants and animals that live on the desert it means simply this: to survive, you must adapt to the amount of water available. The very symbol of the desert, the cactus, is a bundle of marvelous adaptations. Leaves have been reduced to spines, exposing less surface to sunlight. The skin is leathery, thereby letting little water evaporate. The root system can be a broad, shallow net, set near the surface to catch all the water possible and store it (hence "barrel cactus"); or roots can go deep, searching for water below. Desert trees, too, tend to have small leaves with leathery surfaces. Some desert plants are even self-pruning. The body of the cholla (pronounced "choy-ya") cactus is segmented, like a string of sausages. In times of drought the plant cuts circulation to the outer segments, which dry or even drop off. This reduces the plant's size (and therefore its need for water) and surface area. (It is also why the cholla is one of the least pleasant cacti to bump into, and why one species is called "jumping cholla." The outer segments, loosely connected, cling easily to anything that brushes against the plant.)

New Mexico desert animals, too, are precisely suited to this dry climate. The mammals are largely nocturnal, avoiding the daytime sun. Some desert rodents never drink water at all; they metabolize it from seeds that seem perfectly dry to humans. Snakes function well in the desert; they are largely nocturnal, and being cold-blooded (not spending energy to keep the body at any particular temperature) they can eat well in the desert, which at best is a sparsely set table. Lizards are a delight to all youngsters visiting the desert for the first time, as they move from sun to shade, adjusting their body temperature, then sit motionless for long periods of time, waiting for some unwary insect to venture in reach of that lightning tongue. New Mexico does not have too little water; it has

Above
Because of its wide distribution and hardy characteristics, the pinõn, a variety of pine, has been selected as New Mexico's state tree. A favorite source of firewood, the pinõn grows slowly in a region with meager rainfall. Courtesy, Department of Development Collection, NMSRCA

Left
Equally at home in the mountains or on the desert, the omniverous coyote is one of New Mexico's most common mammals. NPS

Bottom
For the sightseer, New Mexico provides some of the Southwest's most spectacular scenery. This photograph taken near Los Alamos looks over the mesas west of the Rio Grande toward the high peaks of the Sangre de Cristo range. Courtesy, Los Alamos National Laboratory

Right
Despite its hostile appearance, the diamondback rattlesnake will usually avoid a confrontation if possible. The rattlesnake is an important figure in the myths and rituals of Southwestern Indians. NPS

precisely the right amount of water for what it is—an arid land, where life must adjust to that aridity.

The rivers of New Mexico are relatively few, but it was along those rivers that history came. The major waterway is the Rio Grande. It rises in the Colorado Rockies and flows down through New Mexico, north to south, dividing the state in half, then forming the Texas-Mexico boundary, and ultimately reaching the Gulf of Mexico. In the northern part of the state, the river rushes at the bottom of a tremendous gorge, the scene of yearly whitewater races in modern times. Sometimes it emerges onto the flats and moves lazily for a while, a braided stream scattered across a wide, sandy riverbed, shallow enough to walk across. Then it passes in rough cuts through the mountains, carving its canyon through the debris of the Jemez volcano west of Santa Fe and, further south, along the Fray Cristóbal Mountains (where the river has been dammed to form Elephant Butte Reservoir) and finally crossing into Texas at El Paso. It was this "Great River" that drew Indians to the region and served as the lifeline for the Spaniards. It is a large river in New Mexico terms but often surprises first-time visitors, who usually exclaim, "why, you can walk across it!" Sometimes you can. Its normal pattern used to be one of flood during snowmelt, then a trickle the rest of the year. (Today dams largely control this, but there is still seasonal variation.)

Another good-sized river, the Pecos, rises in the Sangre de Cristos and flows south, roughly parallel to the Rio Grande, across the eastern plains of the state, eventually joining the Rio Grande in Texas. The continental divide comes down the western side of New Mexico, and a few streams—including the Gila in the southwest and the San Juan in the northwest—flow to the Colorado River and ultimately the Gulf of California. Aficionados know some of the other rivers in the state—the Chama has its fans, especially among trout fishermen—but the statistics speak for themselves. New Mexico has 121,666 square miles of surface area, of which a mere 155 square miles is water, nearly all of that artificial reservoirs. Still, a watercourse need not be one of the famous rivers to be of importance to the people along it. Some canyons, particularly those near significant mountain ranges, have small perennial streams. Plants thrive along them; so do animals and, in many cases, that includes humans. Even dry arroyos sometimes run full. (This can be a tragedy for tourists who camp in the broad, sandy bottom of what they take to be a dry canyon.)

Besides mountains, deserts, and rivers, there has been one final craftsman forming the stage for New Mexico's story. The state is a hotbed of volcanism. No mind that there has been no eruption here in recorded history: geologists and historians use different time-scales. For ages the heat and magma of the earth have broken through to the surface in New Mexico. Capulín Mountain, a national park in the state's northeast corner, preserves an enormous, classic cinder cone, and from the top of it the visitor sees that the surrounding terrain is a family of such cones. The whole southwest part of the state is also volcanic, and it was the escaping heat, with its associated steam and gasses, that helped to form minerals that are mined there today. Throughout the state there

One of a cluster of volcanic cinder cones, Capulín Mountain is a familiar landmark for tourists crossing Northeastern New Mexico on U.S. highways 64 and 87. "Capulín" is the Spanish word for chokecherry, a bush that grows abundantly on the slopes of the mountain. NPS

are visible reminders of its violent geologic past. A million years ago the Jemez volcano exploded with a force many times that of Mt. St. Helens, leaving behind the Valle Grande, one of the great calderas of the world. Today it is a cattle ranch, and scientists poke their drill bits down through the earth toward the magma mass that still lies just a few miles down. They hope to heat water and create electricity with the barest fraction of the sleeping giant's power. At Shiprock and Cabezon Peak, lava froze in the throat of dying volcanoes, forming hard rock towers that outlasted the surrounding mountains.

Nor is it over; about the time of Christ, lava squeezed from the earth near modern Grants. That flow, miles wide and thirty miles long, is so fresh it is worth a pair of shoes to hike across it, and it deserves the local nickname "malpaís," or "bad land." A similar flow near Carrizozo is possibly even more recent.

Lava extrusions have discernibly af-

Above
Located west of Santa Fe in the Jemez Mountains, the Valle Grande is one of the world's largest calderas, with an area of 176 square miles. Courtesy, Los Alamos Historical Museum

Right
A favorite subject for artists and photographers, Shiprock is Northwestern New Mexico's most famous natural attraction. Regina Tatum Cooke created this painting as part of the Federal Arts Project. From the R. Vernon Hunter Collection, NMSRCA

Folsom Man depended on great herds of prehistoric buffalo (bison antiquus) for his existence. To secure a supply of meat, hunting parties drove the huge beasts over steep banks or cornered them in arroyos where they could not escape. From the Marjorie F. Lambert Collection, NMSRCA

Each year thousands of visitors come to Southern New Mexico to experience the beautiful and awe-inspiring limestone formations in Carlsbad Caverns. On the surface temperatures are extreme and rainfall sparse, but below ground the caverns are always cool and moist. The area became a national park in 1930. Courtesy, Albuquerque Convention and Visitors Bureau (ACVB)

Known to generations of New Mexicans as "malpaís" (bad land), the state's rugged lava beds have always been hard on footgear and horses' hoofs. Part of the forty-mile-long flow east of Carrizozo is pictured. From the Department of Development Collection, NMSRCA

fected New Mexico's scenery. Lava is extremely resistant to wind and water, and it protects from erosion the softer material over which it has flowed. At the edge of a flow, however, the softer material beneath, exposed to the elements, erodes rapidly, forming a sharp cliff. The resulting mesas, or perfectly flat-topped hills, are a dramatic feature of the state.

The land of New Mexico is a grand stage. The eastern plains are a mature, timeless landscape, an appropriate transition for approaching motorists who may not realize they are following an ancient trail. The green ribbons of the rivers provide relief. The mesas raise their distinctive outlines, while such oddities as the recent lava flows, the Carlsbad Caverns, and the white sands serve as punctuation. The vastness and the scenic drama are well suited to the story that would unfold: the encounter of people with this beautiful but stern land, and with one another.

The First People

It is certain that there were human beings in New Mexico by 10,000 B.C. The mesas and canyons those first people saw would be familiar to New Mexicans today, even down to individual rocks and caves, but the color was different—it was green. The great ice sheets that covered much of North America at that time never came this far south, but their effect came this far. The eastern plains, treeless today, then had shallow lakes surrounded by pine and even spruce trees. Today's Estancia Basin was a lake, as were the Plains of San Augustin.

If someone from today would be surprised at the lush vegetation of the otherwise familiar landscape, he would be astounded at the animals that roamed across it. There were ancient horses (long extinct by the time the Spaniards arrived) and camels, tapirs and sloths, and even great mammoths. With such game it is not surprising that the first human arrivals were big game hunters.

By chance New Mexico has "type sites" (sites where excavation and reports have established the definition of a culture) for several of North America's early Paleoindian population groups. One of the earliest is Sandia Cave, where meager artifacts of "Sandia Man" have been found in a cave high in the Sandia Mountains above modern Albuquerque. Little is known of these people and how they lived.

Clovis Man's type site, a spot near the modern town of Clovis on the eastern plains, contains numerous heavy projectile points made for hunting. These stone points were attached to a spear that was thrown with an "atl-atl," a tool that in effect lengthened the hunter's forearm, enabling him to throw with tremendous force. Clovis Man was here when the mammoths were, and occasionally even managed to kill one of the great animals for food. These early hunters seem to have built rude, temporary brush shelters, often near water where they watched for game coming down to drink, as on the shores of ancient Lake Estancia. These ancient beaches show up on aerial photos as benches around dry basins, and archeologists have learned that that is where to look for remains of Clovis Man.

As the climate changed, then came the dying. Many of the largest animals disappeared. But as great grasslands developed on the prairies, the herd animals thrived, especially the magnificent *Bison antiquus,* a long-horned species which became the larder for Clovis Man's successor, Folsom Man. Near the little town of Folsom is the type site that produced the most famous spearhead of all, the Folsom point. (There Folsom points were found in direct association with the animals they had killed and provided the first proof, since amply confirmed, that man had coexisted with the great Pleistocene animals.) Exquisitely flaked and balanced, the Folsom point has a characteristically concave cross-section created by chipping off a long flake longitudinally on either side. Removing that long flake took considerable skill and is difficult to perform even today. (One wonders what a Folsom craftsman's professional opinion was of his predecessors, as he looked at the more crudely chipped Clovis points he must have occasionally picked up.)

Unlike Clovis Man, who specialized in individual kills, Folsom Man drove whole herds of bison over steep banks, or up narrowing arroyos, or into loose sand, then

CHAPTER II

moved in with lances to finish the job. Butchering was done on the site; by careful examination of the order of bone piles, seeing which bones were thrown on first and which later, archeologist Joe Ben Wheat has been able to determine the actual butchering method.

There were other early hunting groups, many of which have been identified by archeologists who specialize in the period of the Paleoindians. The Paleoindians inhabited the land for at least twenty times longer than the United States has existed. We have never found their physical remains. We do not know what they wore, or what they lived in, and we have absolutely no idea what their language sounded like. But it is clear that situations of frantic activity and danger, each enough to provide a lifetime of stories for a modern adventurer, were a familiar part of their lives. They knew the terror of facing an enormous, wounded animal with just a stone-tipped spear; and some even knew the taste of mammoth meat, an animal we shall never even see.

By about 6000 B.C. New Mexico was beginning to display the characteristic browns and reds that attract visitors today (actually a sign of aridity). The great variety of New Mexico's landforms created a range of environments, from moist canyon heads to high timber, from sandy desert and stands of seemingly inhospitable cactus to large areas of pinon trees. To live in this new situation, people learned to use all of these environments. They spread into the canyon heads and the valleys, learning when and where to look for food, when to return to areas with ripening grass seed, and where to find a spring that might still drip a little water.

Life in the Archaic period (approximately 6000 to 1000 B.C.) was quite different from that which had been enjoyed by Paleoindians (10,000 to 6000 B.C.). The herds were gone, now moving east across the great plains. The remaining humans found it necessary to know one area very well and to glean from a variety of its sources. New Mexicans of the Archaic period were hunters and gatherers, moving season by season to where the resources were ripening. The tools Paleoindians left behind are for hunting and butchering big game; Archaic "tool kits" have stone tools for grinding seeds, and projectile points, knives, and scrapers suitable for hunting and preparing a variety of small game.

The achievements that would make it possible for people to master this arid environment probably were not recognized as remarkable at the time. Corn, which would revolutionize their lives one day, probably came in as a handful of seed traded from people who might have migrated slowly, generation by generation, northward from Mexico. You could plant it in some likely spot on your travels and harvest it next time around, if the birds had not found it first. Or you could leave someone there to scare the birds away, so that. . . . There was the revolution: a nomadic people of hunters and gatherers were going to become farmers, accomplishing the unprecedented feat of living in one place. It would take millenia to put the inventions, techniques, and combinations into place to make it work.

With the development of agriculture came the period of what archeologists refer to as the Basketmaker (roughly 1000 B.C. to A.D. 800). At some point people invented nets for catching rabbits and improved tumplines for carrying loads. They modified and improved stone tools that had originally been used for grinding wild seed. Beans and squash became part of the diet. Gradually these New Mexicans began to acquire new skills, again probably from Mexico. They made pottery and cooked in it, grew and used cotton, mastered the bow and arrow, and began building storage cists.

The idea of storing one crop, rather than searching for another, was an important step. Pottery served the purpose, but storage cists, specially designed holes in the floor, had greater size and permanence. Finally, the tendency to stay in one place made it sensible to spend more time building a house for year-round living, rather than the seasonal brush shelters of the nomad. Thus was invented the pithouse, which in one form or another would house perhaps half of all the people who lived in New Mexico before the coming of the Spaniards. It was usually but not always round, was built partially underground, and usually had a ramp entranceway or a hatch and ladder. The roof was made of poles, brush, and dirt. Outside a home like this would be a work area for scraping skins, sewing, chipping spearheads, and grinding grain. Here, too, a Basketmaker could sit in the evening, talk with his neighbors, and chew the native tobacco. Archeologists have found the quids.

The Basketmaker period had much of the Archaic in it, but it was Archaic-plus-corn, and that made a profound difference. Small groups of semi-nomads became farmers living in pithouse villages, with food stored from good years to even out the bad ones.

Having moved from brush shelters on the surface to pithouses underground, the people of New Mexico now came back to the surface again. The first above-ground

Above
Modern-day craftsmen would likely envy the skill of the Anasazi masons who built the Chaco villages. The same people also constructed a remarkable road system at Chaco, but its purpose is not clear. NPS

Left
Because of its astonishing size, pueblo Bonito is the best known of several Anasazi villages in Chaco Canyon. Its residents were traders who also practiced irrigated farming. To insure its preservation, Chaco Canyon is now a national historic park. Courtesy, State Historic Preservation Bureau (SHPB)

Arroyo Hondo, located five miles south of Santa Fe, was a large multistoried pueblo occupied during the thirteenth and early fourteenth centuries. Archeologists from the School of American Research in Santa Fe first investigated the site in 1971. Because of long habitation by prehistoric peoples, New Mexico is rich in archeological resources. From the School of American Research Collection, NMSRCA

structures of rock and mud began to appear in the seventh and eighth centuries and were evidently used for storage. Eventually, the above-ground houses came to predominate. The ancient pithouse did not disappear entirely, but was transformed into the kiva, a ceremonial structure. Centuries later the Spaniards would find New Mexico's Indians living in rock and mud houses with adjacent kivas. Creating a term that exists yet today, they called the natives "Pueblos." Today the term is applied to the building itself, the village, the individual, and the culture. The term is also used for the period of development that began around A.D. 800.

The most elaborate and intriguing of New Mexico's early pueblos are found at Chaco Canyon. At the middle of the tenth century Chaco contained a typical mix of pithouses and masonry houses, and a relatively large population, but was not vastly different from other centers of the pueblo group we now call Anasazi. But sometime around A.D. 950, building construction began at an accelerated rate. At first the buildings had essentially the same floor plan as was already common, but writ large: the rooms were twice as big, there were more of them, and a second story might be added. The surge did not stop but carried over generations, culminating in the marvel of Pueblo Bonito, a five-story, 800-room building designed as a harmonious D-shaped whole, containing its own plaza and more than thirty kivas. The masonry technique changed from generation to generation, but some of it is the finest anywhere, with banded effects deliberately created by skillful placement of rock. Eleven of these extraordinarily large, well-built towns are found in the immediate vicinity of Chaco Canyon.

More astonishing still are the enigmatic lines across the countryside that show up clearly on aerial photographs, radiating from Chaco Canyon. Studies have confirmed that these are indeed a network of roadways, built by people who had neither the wheel nor beasts of burden. More than 460 miles of road have been traced so far. They lead to other outlying towns that have Chaco-type architecture. These towns, more than seventy-five identified so far, had some tie back to Chaco Canyon, either political, economic, religious, or cultural.

Chaco Canyon does not fit the mold of Pueblo societies, at least as they are understood now. Such societies usually are egalitarian; at Chaco there are hints of rich folks and poor folks, as finer artifacts are found in the large structures than in the small ones. The architecture is unique, the roads are unique, and the size of the "system," whatever it was, linking towns spread over the San Juan drainage, was unprecedented. There are theories, of course. One is based on the extreme variability of growing conditions in the Chaco area. It is difficult to predict whether a given year will produce a crop or not, and even if one place does, an area a few miles away may be parched. The way to cope with shortages over time is by storage, and the way to cope with shortages in different places is by transfer. The huge rooms at

Chaco could be storage, and the roads could be transfer. Could Chaco have been administering a food redistribution system, to smooth out the unpredictabilities of farming a marginal area?

The reasons for Chaco's decline are not clear, although probably they involved multiple blows of drought and failures of the "system," whatever it was. Quite rapidly, between 1150 and 1200, construction ceased and the population declined radically. It was just about then that the cliff towns at Mesa Verde, 100 miles to the north, were approaching their zenith in population and activity, and it is attractive (and easy) to think of skilled Chacoans moving up there to touch off a great advance. Furthermore, when Mesa Verde declined around 1300, there was a blossoming of the pueblos in the Rio Grande Valley. Did the same crew move over there? Some have guessed so, but probably the truth is more complex. In fact, cultures rarely move in jumps. The better metaphor might be the braided stream, like the Rio Grande. Look over the bridge in Albuquerque. Water moves within the broad sand bed from one side to the other—a trickle here and a solid stream over there which then changes and moves to a new arrangement of deep and shallow places. Some pools even become isolated to one side, possibly to disappear. It seems even so in the family of cultures.

Meanwhile, in the southern part of the state, a sister culture to the Anasazi was the Mogollón. It may have been the Mogollón who had introduced pottery and even the idea of pithouses to the Anasazi, and in at least one way they exceeded even Chaco: the Mimbres offshoot of the Mogollón produced the finest potters of prehistoric times. By the late 1200s the northern Mogollón had become the innovative ceramic center of the Southwest, but by the mid-1400s the Mogollón had abandoned most of their homes in southwestern New Mexico.

Even as the Anasazi and the Mogollón, the people of the northern Rio Grande

One of the most intriguing archeological sites in New Mexico, the Gila Cliff Dwellings are located forty-four miles north of Silver City. The cliff houses were built in a series of natural caves and occupied by farming people in the thirteenth and fourteenth centuries. The monument also contains pit houses made by an earlier Mogollón culture about A.D. 100 to 400. From the Marjorie F. Lambert Collection, NMSRCA

These artifacts include examples of the geometric designs and living creatures that characterize Mimbres pottery. The exhibit is part of the Eisele Collection at the University of New Mexico's Maxwell Museum. From the Calvin Collection. Courtesy, University of New Mexico General Libary, Special Collections

Right
Hollowed-out caves sheltered some Frijoles residents. They were a farming people who raised corn, beans, and squash, and also made pottery. NPS

Below
Some of the most significant archeological sites in the Northern Rio Grande Valley are situated in Bandelier National Monument, west of Santa Fe. Photo by Fred Mang, Jr., NPS

Estancia Valley's salt lakes are vestiges of a much larger body of water, which covered the area during prehistoric times. Salt gathered at the lakes was an important trade item for nearby Pueblo Indians. After the Spanish conquest, large quantities of the salt were sent to New Spain for use in a silver extraction process. NPS

passed through the pithouse and small pueblo stages. Evidently they were influenced by the Anasazi in the Chaco area, and later by ideas from the Mesa Verde area. By the late 1200s and early 1300s these people lived in adobe or masonry pueblos, usually located on tributaries to the Rio Grande or somctimes near the great river itself. Some of these towns grew to great size, but there was much moving around and, oddly, even large towns were often abandoned, sometimes for reasons that today's archeologists cannot figure out. This common abandoning of villages may be more understandable if we realize that we are sedentary and accept living in one place as the "right" way of things. Recently nomadic people may need as much reason to stay as we do to move.

Some of these pueblo towns, including Taos, Picurís, and Pecos, engaged in extensive trade, especially with the non-pueblo Indians to the east. There nomads, who would come to be known as Apaches and Navajos, lived by hunting the bison on the grasslands. The nomads had meat but no corn, hides but no cotton clothing. The farmer-Pueblos living in the Rio Grande Valley and near it were quick to meet the needs of the Plains Indians on the other side of the mountains just to the east; so just beyond Glorieta Pass and further south—near Abo Pass—towns developed on the east side of the mountains that specialized in trade with the plains.

The scene in New Mexico was vastly different from the distant, hazy days when big game learned to fear men with spears; there was even a pueblo that traded salt from the desiccated bed of what had been Lake Estancia. Towns had been built, usually square, often one large building surrounding three sides of a plaza. There were shifting political and economic alliances. Art forms were recognizable as being from one region or another. Jewelry was being manufactured and traded. Life was well-ordered, and from what we know of Pueblo culture later, customs were entrenched. Profoundly complicated and meaningful ceremonies happened at predictable times, necessary to keep the universe functioning properly and—specifically—to make the corn grow. Old people told children the stories of the tribe (although this probably happened in Pleistocene times as well). One wonders what this culture might have done, what direction its development might have taken, if history had taken a different turn. But it was 1492, and a tidal wave was gathering in a distant sea. Soon it would engulf New Mexico.

During the reign of Philip II, a contract for the colonization of New Mexico was granted to Juan de Oñate, scion of a Zacatecas mining family. Philip died two months after Oñate established his headquarters at the Indian village of Ohke on the Rio Grande. From the Long Collection, NMSRCA

Spanish Explorers

It was a long international history that finally brought a handful of Spaniards trudging into New Mexico. In the hindsight of history books, their coming has a sense almost of inevitability, but from the view of the Indians already living among the canyons and mesas, it was the unexpected bordering on the unbelievable. One suspects that the first word came as rumors from the far south, of men known to us as Columbus and Cortez. After the conquest of Central America, it was an ill-fated expedition led by Pánfilo de Narváez that first brought New Mexico to the attention of Spain. The expedition was a disaster, and only four of its members survived, turning up eight years and thousands of miles later on the northwest coast of Mexico to report a series of remarkable adventures. It is unlikely that these men had actually entered New Mexico. They had struck west from the Rio Grande, some distance below present-day El Paso, toward Sonora. Nevertheless they had heard of Indian towns north of their route, with multi-storied buildings and great riches. These vague rumors of lands-almost-seen had a dramatic effect on the restless and ambitious Spaniards who inhabited the New World outposts of the empire.

To check out the stories, Viceroy Antonio de Mendoza sent a small scouting expedition, in the charge of Fray Marcos de Niza but actually led by one of the survivors, a Moorish slave named Estevan. Desert-hardened Estevan pushed on ahead of the friar until he reached the pueblo of Hawikuh, one of a cluster of small Zuni Indian villages south of present-day Gallup. There Estevan was killed. Exactly how close Fray Marcos came to Hawikuh, or what he saw, is not clear. In any case the Spaniards in Mexico were convinced that there were riches to be had in the tantalizing lands beyond the wild desert which up to now had blocked them from the north. After all, had they not found unexpected riches in Mexico and Peru?

Competition began immediately among the leading men of Mexico, each clamoring to be allowed to gamble his own fortune to lead a northward expedition. The man finally chosen was Francisco Vásquez de Coronado—young, wealthy, well-connected, and governor of the province of Nueva Galicia. The expedition assembled at Compostela, capital of Nueva Galicia, some 800 miles north of Mexico City, and on February 22, 1540, it started north.

There were perhaps 1,200 people, all but 336 of them natives, with more than 1,000 mounts and pack animals and a herd of food animals—cattle, goats, and sheep.

From a centuries-later viewpoint, an expedition seems to be all newness and adventure; it is easy to overlook the sheer physical labor of it. Everything needed by a large group of people had to be carried, every day. Even if carried by a horse, it was pulled down and lifted up as many times a day as necessary. Shovels, clothes, axes, armor, weapons, ammunition, medicines, food, records, spare parts, cooking gear—all of it was hauled north. Just the process of living during the trek took labor. Firewood had to be cut and gathered, water carried. A shelter did not just "appear": it had to be put up and taken down. Animals had to be saddled and unsaddled, packed and unpacked, and tended to. Bedding was not just slept in: it was carried, laid out, and packed up again.

CHAPTER III

In August of 1540 the forces of conquistador Francisco Vásquez de Coronado first encountered New Mexico's Zuni Indians before the pueblo of Hawikuh. Coronado's army, composed of 300 soldiers and 800 friendly Indians, had marched north from New Spain to explore the fabled "Seven Cities of Cíbola." This colorful representation of Coronado's encounter was painted by Gerald P. Cassidy. NMSRCA

Rivers were swollen, and not one of them was easy to cross. But the army we would call a mob trudged north. The history books say the medieval age was over, but it seemed that here was a piece of it: Coronado in his gilded armor (which must have been an oven on the desert, one presumes used for reviews and combat but not for marching), leading men with arms that any farmer in Europe would have recognized—lances, swords, bows and arrows, and just a few potent, expensive crossbows and arquebusses. As the purpose was exploration and possibly conquest, but not colonization, there were but a dozen or fewer women. And because this was a Spanish expedition of the sixteenth century, there were friars, four identified in the records and several others unnamed, to succor the souls of their countrymen and identify mission fields in the area they would explore. One of them was Marcos de Niza, who had led the first tentative foray with the unfortunate Estevan.

After a trek of nearly six months, the expedition reached Hawikuh—Fray Marcos' gilded city—and found it a miserable collection of stone-and-mud houses. Its people neither came out to trade nor invited the explorers into busy marketplaces; instead they resisted. The Spaniards attacked. Neither side had weapons we would consider formidable today. Coronado himself was downed temporarily by a well-aimed stone, his plumed helmet perhaps offering an easy target for Indian marksmen. The fight was short, and the Spaniards prevailed. Europeans had arrived in New Mexico.

Hope dies hard. When pressed, the Indians of Hawikuh told of other cities and, yes, those cities were rich. Coronado split his forces. He sent one detachment west to search for rumored towns in that direction. It found the Hopi villages, sitting in the sun on their timeless mesas. Another detachment, under Captain Hernando de Alvarado, was sent east with an Indian guide known as Bigotes, so called because of his mustache, unusual for an Indian. (Bigotes had arrived at Hawikuh as the leader of a delegation from Pecos, on the eastern fringe of the Pueblo country, sent to investigate the incredible report of the Spaniards' arrival.) In early September 1540 Bigotes led a group of perhaps two dozen Spaniards back toward his homeland. They were the first Europeans to enter

the Rio Grande Valley, the heart of the Pueblo region then, and the heart of New Mexico now.

They reached Acoma, the "Sky City," then swung north and east. The trudging soldiers welcomed the long downslope that brought them to a great river. It was the Rio Grande, which they reached at approximately the site of Albuquerque today. The area was heavily settled even then, for Bigotes had brought them to the heart of the Pueblo country. From there north were numerous Indian towns set amongst fields along the river. Alvarado records that representatives from twelve such towns came to meet him, bringing gifts. He called the "kingdom" (for he could think only as a European) Tiguex.

From there the Spaniards ranged northward to the Jemez, San Juan, and Taos pueblos. Time has been relatively kind to Taos, and today's visitor can, with a little effort, blank out the modern additions and see approximately what Alvarado's little band saw. Of course the two great buildings were eyeless then, for windows came later; but still they sit solidly on opposite sides of the stream that comes down from the massive sacred mountain that protects the village. By then winter was coming on, and the Spaniards retreated to near present-day Bernalillo. From there Alvarado sent riders to Coronado, still at Hawikuh, with this message: bring the army here for the winter; there are warm rooms and corn.

After dispatching the report to Coronado, Alvarado's band pushed eastward toward Pecos and the plains beyond, hoping to find the great herds of buffalo of which Bigotes and his men had told Coronado. They entered the narrow western opening of Glorieta Pass and descended on the other side to the pueblo of Pecos. There they rested and enjoyed the hospitality of Bigotes' home village, but Alvarado was anxious to find the bison herds and decided to push on. Bigotes remained at Pecos, and the Spaniards took as guides two Plains Indians—captives being held as slaves at Pecos—known as "the Turk" and Sopete.

The group found the great animals in only four days. Now that bison have been reduced to such miserably few numbers, and virtually everyone knows what they look like, it may be hard to recreate the effect of that first encounter. "The most

The Zuni Indians were astonished by the Spaniards' horses and armor. In 1921 Santa Fe artist Gerald P. Cassidy painted this triptych, which depicts the first meeting between Francisco Vásquez de Coronado and New Mexico's indigenous people. The painting now hangs in Santa Fe's Federal Building. NMSRCA

monstrous beasts we have ever seen or heard about," wrote Alvarado, and so multitudinous that he "did not know to what to compare them unless it be to the fish of the sea." But soon the wonder of the bison was replaced by erroneous reports of an even greater wonder, the one the Spaniards had come so far to find: gold.

More than four centuries later it is impossible to know just what the Turk had in mind. The captive may simply have wanted the Spaniards to take him to Quivira, his homeland in what we now call Kansas, or he may have intended to lure them to their deaths on the plains. Perhaps he just enjoyed making a sensation. At any rate the Turk soon discovered the Spaniards' preoccupation with gold and told them that the metal abounded in his homeland. As evidence he claimed that he had had a gold bracelet when captured, that it had been taken from him, and that even now it was in the possession of none other than Bigotes.

If the Turk wanted to create a sensation, he certainly succeeded. The tiny army, having seen the buffalo, turned around and returned to Pecos. There they questioned Bigotes, who denied the story. The cacique, or religious leader of the Pecos, backed Bigotes' denial. But belief is born of desire, and the Spaniards wanted very much to believe. Bigotes, the cacique, the Turk, and Sopete were all taken in chains back to Tiguex, where Alvarado expected to meet Coronado and the main army. Here indeed was news for the general.

Alvarado and his prisoners arrived at Tiguex to find that Coronado had not yet arrived but had sent Captain García López de Cárdenas with an advance detachment to prepare the way. To be fair to

For centuries, Pueblo women have baked in beehive-shaped ovens called "hornos." Their tasty bread has always been a popular item wherever Indian arts and crafts are displayed. From the Woodward Collection, NMSRCA

Above
Europeans first visited Taos in 1540, during an exploration of the northern pueblos made by Coronado's Captain Hernando de Alvarado. The party's scribe reported multistoried apartment houses made of adobe, a description that still fits today. SHPS

Left
Coronado's men first saw buffalo when they ventured onto the plains east of the Pecos River. There they also met the Querechos, an Apache group who followed the great herds, carrying their hide tepees on dog travois. From the WPA Collection, NMSRCA

Cárdenas, there is evidence that the Spaniards began to prepare their own quarters for winter, but soon the cold set in, and time was short. Cárdenas then "asked" the Indians—the verb is in the records but not enlarged upon—simply to move out of one of their villages and let the Spaniards move in. The Indians left, and the Spaniards moved into the pueblo called Alcanfor to wait for Coronado and the rest of the army.

On the very night Coronado arrived—after a hard march from Hawikuh, by way of El Morro, and up the Rio Grande—the Turk confirmed everything, adding more and more embellishments. Coronado checked with Bigotes and the cacique from Pecos, who continued to deny the existence of the golden bracelet. To make them tell the "truth," apparently the Spaniards' fierce war dogs were used to harass or at least frighten the Pecos witnesses. They stuck to their story, but they would not forget the dog baiting.

The winter was cold and hard. Relations between Spaniards and Indians in the Rio Grande Valley, which had begun hospitably, disintegrated in the hard winter. Coronado sent parties to ask the Indians for food and supplies. Apparently Coronado sincerely wanted to obtain the supplies without bloodshed, but the wish was fantastic. Somebody had to be hungry, and it was not clear to those who had farmed just why it should be they.

The climax came with the horses. Fascinating to the Indians, the huge animals gave the Spaniards almost miraculous mobility. Whether out of curiosity about the animals or in retaliation for the levies, the Indians staged a raid on the herd. Tracing their tracks to a pueblo called Arenal, the Spaniards saw the Indians driving the horses around the plaza, shooting them with arrows. An attempt at diplomacy failed, and the inevitable battle was fierce. The Indians barricaded themselves in their pueblo, which was a formidable defense against the arms of the Spaniards. The Spaniards broke through the mud walls and built smudge fires to force the Indians out. There was terrifying hand-to-hand combat in the dark, smoky rooms, but in the end the struggle became a rout. Possibly because of a mix-up in orders, Indians who thought they had been promised amnesty for surrendering were tied to stakes and burned. The witnesses from Pecos observed it all.

The Battle of Arenal took place at the end of December 1540, and despite the harshness of winter, nearby Indians abandoned their towns and fled into the Sandia Mountains. The Spaniards—learning that the Indians were reassembling in a village called Moho, somewhere above present-day Bernalillo—laid siege to the pueblo. The siege lasted six weeks. The Indians tried to dig a well, but it caved in, killing thirty. With sorrow as old as warfare, they turned over their women and children to the besiegers, hoping for safety for them, and attempted a last, desperate breakout. It was futile. The mounted Spaniards rode them down, lancing them from horseback, and many died trying to swim the frigid waters of the Rio Grande. A tragic pattern had been set and confirmed.

Finally it was spring, and on April 23, 1541, Coronado set out to pursue the golden dreams fostered and fed by the Turk. They crossed the frozen Rio Grande, passed through Glorieta Pass, and reached Pecos. Somehow, now or earlier, the tales of the Turk meshed with a plot by the leaders at Pecos to destroy the Spaniards or at least get rid of them by leading them far out onto thc plains. Unaware, Coronado and his men pushed on across the plains, land as flat and featureless as the sea.

Like Alvarado's reconnaissance before them, they found the great larder of the plains, the buffalo. The huge animals were in herds of numbers that staggered the imagination. The expedition encountered bands of Plains Indians who followed the herds, killing and butchering the animals very much as their Paleoindian ancestors had done 100 centuries earlier. The Spaniards had found one of the wonders and treasures of the (future) American West—one that would soon be squandered—but it was not the treasure they sought.

At last it became apparent that the Turk's story was not holding up. Alvarado noted that the Turk's directions were not the same as they had been the previous autumn, and there were discrepancies, too, with what the nomadic buffalo hunters told them. The continued protests of Sopete and Bigotes, who claimed all along that the Turk was lying, may have begun to sink in. In any case there was a confrontation—one wishes the record offered more detail, for it must have been dramatic—and the Turk confessed. He had lied. The houses of his people were only of grass. He had wanted not only to return to his own people but also to get the Spaniards lost on the empty plains.

Coronado decided to send the main part of his army back to Tiguex, while proceeding himself with thirty selected men to investigate this rapidly diminishing Quivira. There was a parting on the plains. The main body returning enlisted some of the Plains Indians as guides to shorten the return trip. The Spaniards were fascinated by the method their guides used. Each morning, taking bearings by the sunrise, the Indians shot an arrow as far as possible in the appropriate direction. They then traveled toward the arrow, but, before

During the autumn of 1540, Coronado established winter quarters among Pueblo Indians living in the Rio Grande Valley. The village of Kuaua, recently excavated and restored, may have been the site chosen by the adventurers. The Spaniards called the area Tiguex because the natives belonged to the Tiwa linguistic group. ACVB

For the Pueblo Indians, the kiva *was an important center of their religious life. Conversely, Spaniards hated and feared these underground chambers as the sources of pagan practices. During times of repression, civil and religious authorities frequently ordered their destruction. NPS*

they reached it, shot another arrow past it and walked toward that one, thereby achieving a straight line of travel.

Meanwhile Coronado and his detachment pushed on, the vindicated Sopete now in the lead and the Turk in chains. In a month of travel, any day of which would be in today's terms a tremendous adventure—or an hour in a car—they reached Quivira. Where they had hoped for golden chandeliers, they found straw huts. Secretly (for they were in the Turk's land) they strangled and buried the Turk. Then they began the long journey back to Tiguex to rejoin the rest of the army.

By this time the main unit—which had reached Tiguex—had realized Pecos' involvement in the plot to lose the Spaniards on the plains and went to Pecos to wait for Coronado, figuring that their force could prevent the powerful Pecos pueblo from attempting to wipe his unit out. They were right, and Coronado successfully rejoined his main army. But the success was a hollow one. Winter was at hand, and the expedition could not return to Mexico. They would have to spend another winter at Tiguex, with nothing but the empty-handed return to look forward to in the spring.

At least two and possibly three of the friars elected to stay in the mission field they had discovered. Fray Juan de Padilla returned to Quivira; Luis de Escalona stayed at Pecos; and it seems that a third stayed in Tiguex. The latter two soon found the martyrdom they evidently sought. Though it took a little longer, so did Padilla, who met his death, kneeling, in a shower of arrows. This is known from the eyewitness account of his Portuguese servant, Andrés de Campo, who was taken prisoner but escaped and ultimately made his way back to Mexico five years later.

By then Coronado's expedition was long gone from New Mexico. The army that had descended dramatically on the land gathered its wondrous horses, its metal, its gunpowder, and, leaving behind a small taste of its religion and a branded memory of its power and will, walked back past Acoma, past Hawikuh, and disappeared to the south.

It was two generations before another band of explorers probed north from New Spain into the Pueblo country. The delay was significant, for during it the Council of the Indies in Spain, acting in the name of the Crown, instituted the Ordinances of 1573. The New World experience was presenting new problems for Europe—problems of administration, finance, logistics, even of morality. A vocal faction led by the church had raised serious questions about the treatment of the native peoples. The Ordinances of 1573 reflected a new view. There was to be no "conquest"—the very word was forbidden. A permit from the king was necessary to undertake "pacification," and the rights of Indians were enumerated. Still, the northern frontier of New Spain (what are today the Mexican states just below the Texas-Mexico border) was far from the heartland of the rapidly growing colony that centered on the capital in Mexico City. It was a tough mining frontier, and distant rules bent easily.

In one "boom" town called Santa Bárbara, a particularly devout Franciscan lay brother named Agustín Rodríguez yearned for the mission field rumored to exist to the north. There is no evidence that he knew anything about Coronado's journey two generations before, but he worked with local Indians, and some of them had told him about other Indians to the north. He applied for permission to go north. His band was to receive a military escort of nine soldiers, led by Captain Francisco Sánchez Chamuscado and including one Hernan Gallegos, who would keep a journal (and thus earn the gratitude of historians).

The party left Santa Bárbara on June 5, 1581. Chamuscado may have escorted the friars, but he did not seem overly concerned with their mission. As they entered New Mexico coming up the Rio Grande, he began "taking possession" for the king. The little band ranged the pueblos between present-day Albuquerque and Galisteo Creek, going west to Zuni and east to Pecos and into the plains, but the soldiers were more interested in mineral deposits than Indian souls. One of the friars, Fray Juan de Santa María, was determined to report the subversion of the expedition and left to walk back to Mexico. When the soldiers finally decided to return, the two other friars elected to stay at a pueblo somewhere near present-day Bernalillo.

Captain Chamuscado died of natural causes before the soldiers got back to Santa Bárbara, but the survivors brought back stories of towns to the north worthy of colonization. The buzz that followed was like the one that had followed Fray Marcos' return forty years before, this time with the added touch of concern for the friars who had stayed behind.

In the midst of the buzz was Antonio de Espejo, who with his brother owned successful ranching and mining enterprises in northern New Spain. Temporarily out of favor with the authorities, Espejo was in the north to escape legal difficulties in Mexico City. Here was a chance for a daring man to recoup all in one triumph: he would use his wealth to sponsor a rescue attempt of the friars left behind in the north. In deliberate confusion as to whether he had permission or not, he set out on March 10, 1582, with a small expedition, and once again Spaniards were traveling up the Rio Grande.

The fate of one of the friars had been learned already. Fray Santa María, the one who had set out to walk to Mexico, had never finished his lonely journey. Trudging south through the Estancia Valley, he had stopped and stretched out to rest; Indians killed him where he lay. As for the other two who had stayed behind, Espejo learned that they also had been killed. Having discovered their fate, the soldiers wanted nevertheless to go on. They visited the pueblos, confirming once again that these were not opulent, European-style towns.

Nonetheless, on their return to Mexico there was the predictable uproar of speculation. This time the buzz was loud enough to reach the Crown, and the search began for an official colonizer. In the meantime, however, there would be at least one more ragtag unofficial probe.

This most unlikely expedition of all was that of Gaspar Castaño de Sosa, lieutenant governor of the province of New León and part-time slaver. In a moment of vaunting imagination, he persuaded the whole population of his tiny colonial settlement, some 200 strong, to remove with him to the outback in direct contravention of a viceregal order. They brought wheeled carts, the first ever seen in New Mexico. Their decision to travel up the Pecos was a mistake, for the terrain was broken and rough. There were armed encounters—precisely what the Crown had wished to avoid—and a pursuing expedition caught up with de Sosa at the pueblo of Santa Domingo. De Sosa was returned to Mexico in irons (although he was later pardoned). The Crown was now ready for an official attempt.

A swaggering nobleman, Diego José de Vargas Zapata y Luján Ponce de León y Contreras—known as Diego de Vargas—is the hero of the reconquest of New Mexico. During a 1692 reconnaissance he personally persuaded Pueblo leaders to accept a Spanish return. When he came back in 1693 with colonists and Franciscans, he was compelled to quell Indian resistance by force. This portrait of Diego de Vargas hangs in the Museum of New Mexico. Courtesy, Museum of New Mexico (MNM) (#11409)

Colonization and Conquest

The man chosen to lead an expedition to colonize, not merely explore, the distant north was Juan de Oñate, son of a wealthy mine operator in Zacatecas. Oñate offered to finance the expedition himself. In return he was to receive a hereditary governorship, along with various other titles and an immense land grant on the new frontier.

On January 7, 1598, the caravan of 130 men, their wives and children, ten Franciscan friars, and an immense herd of bawling animals started north. They traveled on foot, on horseback, and in ox-drawn carts. Instead of following the rivers as others had done, Oñate decided to strike north, straight across the desert, to intercept the Rio Grande where it swung to the east. Unknowingly he finished blazing the Camino Real into New Mexico, a road that one day would carry the commerce of the United States and Mexico—two countries that did not yet exist.

The Pass—"Paso del Norte"—where the river shouldered its way between mountains and where one also had to ford the river, was generally accepted as the entrance to New Mexico, and somewhere on the Rio Grande near there Oñate and the friars performed an elaborate civil and religious ceremony of claiming the region, a ceremony which included the medieval custom of tossing grass and stones into the air. From a nearby hillside a curious Indian pausing to watch would have found it comic: tiny, ant-like figures in the immensity of New Mexico, claiming in a puny voice, lost in the wind, land, riches, and souls for God and king. The souls and riches would prove elusive, and in just twelve years Oñate himself would return the same way, a broken man. But do not disdain that impertinence along the Rio Grande. In some ways the Spaniards made their claim stick. Some four centuries later this land still bears the rich stamp of Spain in customs, food, architecture, and language.

The Spaniards crossed the river and followed it north, seeing with immeasurably more time and curiosity the scenery a motorist sees today hurrying north on I-25 from El Paso. Indians were few, and the land a desert. Near the present-day improbably named town of Truth or Consequences they were forced by rough terrain to the east side of the Caballo and Fray Cristóbal mountain ranges, across a ninety-mile stretch without water or shade. A man named Robledo died at the beginning of the crossing—a small settlement still bears his name. This area is still known as the Jornada del Muerto (Dead Man's Journey).

The caravan reached the Piro Indian villages, causing most of the natives to flee. There the Spaniards paused and rested, eating corn given them by the few Indians who stayed behind. Further north were more villages, and the expedition found welcome relief around present-day Socorro.

At the pueblo called Santa Domingo, north of Bernalillo, there was a happy discovery. Two of the Mexican Indians left behind by Castaño de Sosa's expedition were still there. For seven years they had lived among these river farmers, and they spoke the local tongue. Here the Spaniards were met by seven "chiefs" (a strictly European concept) whom Oñate somehow understood to represent thirty-four villages. This was impossible, but the Spaniards didn't know it and were gratified as

CHAPTER IV

For centuries New Mexicans depended on ox carts called "carretas" to bring supplies of all kinds north from New Spain. In the seventeenth century the Franciscans organized and directed supply caravans. This example of a carreta of more recent vintage is on display at the Museum of New Mexico. From the School of American Research Collection, NMSRCA

the representatives swore allegiance to the God and king of Spain. The capabilities of the translators must have been sorely strained.

On July 11, 1598, the expedition reached the end of its journey, near present-day Espanola. There, where the Chama empties into the Rio Grande, near the pueblo today called San Juan, Oñate and his advance party established the first Spanish headquarters in New Mexico. A month later the main caravan, which the group had left behind, arrived at the fledgling colony.

The story of the Oñate colony is usually told in the actions of its leader, especially the extraordinary trips he took. With a retinue of soldiers and friars, he traveled on horseback through Glorieta Pass to Pecos and out onto the plains. He went to the area around present-day Mountainair and, as usual, conducted elaborate ceremonies to accept the allegiance of the pueblos. In one astonishing journey he crossed Arizona to the mouth of the Colorado. On the way back he paused at the ancient watering hole at the foot of the great rock of El Morro and carved into the rock his name and the date: April 16, 1606.

But just as important as the peripatetic travels of their leader were the experiences and gradual disillusionment of the colonists. Ordinarily a frontier settlement is at the edge of the unknown; just behind it is the known, providing support. But this fledgling colony had leap-frogged 1,500 miles from the colonial heartland. It was a "bubble" frontier, with little or no support. And now winter hit hard, longer and colder than these people from the south had expected. Their crops did badly. The cold dry hills turned out to be just dry hills, with no gold or silver hidden in them.

As for the Indians, some Spaniards saw them as souls to be won, and others disdained them, but probably all underestimated them. Juan de Zaldívar, Oñate's nephew, paid for just this mistake with his life. Sent to Acoma to procure food, he and most of his men were wiped out in an ambush. The Spanish reacted ferociously. Vicente de Zaldívar, younger brother of the slain officer, was sent with seventy soldiers to avenge the deaths. They were brutally successful and brought back more than 500 prisoners—men, women, and children—nearly all sentenced to slavery.

Other conflicts followed, and discontent grew. The missionary effort was drawn back from outlying pueblos and concentrated along the Rio Grande; even there it was often frustrated. Reading the record today it appears that the Spaniards failed to understand the Indians' polytheism, which made them quite willing to adopt the new religion while steadfastly keeping the old. Religious and economic frustrations mounted. The colony dwindled under mass desertions, and in the end Oñate himself began the long trek back to Mexico. His fortune was lost to the defeated enterprise, and all hope of glory was gone.

This turning point in New Mexico history brought a remarkable decision by the Spanish Crown. The New Mexico colony had proved unprofitable, but a missionary effort had begun and could not be aban-

Left
Oñate established his first headquarters on the east bank of the Rio Grande at the Indian village of Ohke. Within a few months the settlers moved across the river to Yuqueyunque (pictured). MNM (#16739)

Below
Oñate left an inscription chiseled in the soft rock at El Morro. Translated into English the inscription reads: "Adelantado don Juan de Oñate passed this way from the discovery of the South Sea, April 16, 1606" (actually 1605). Courtesy, State Parks and Recreation, NMSRCA

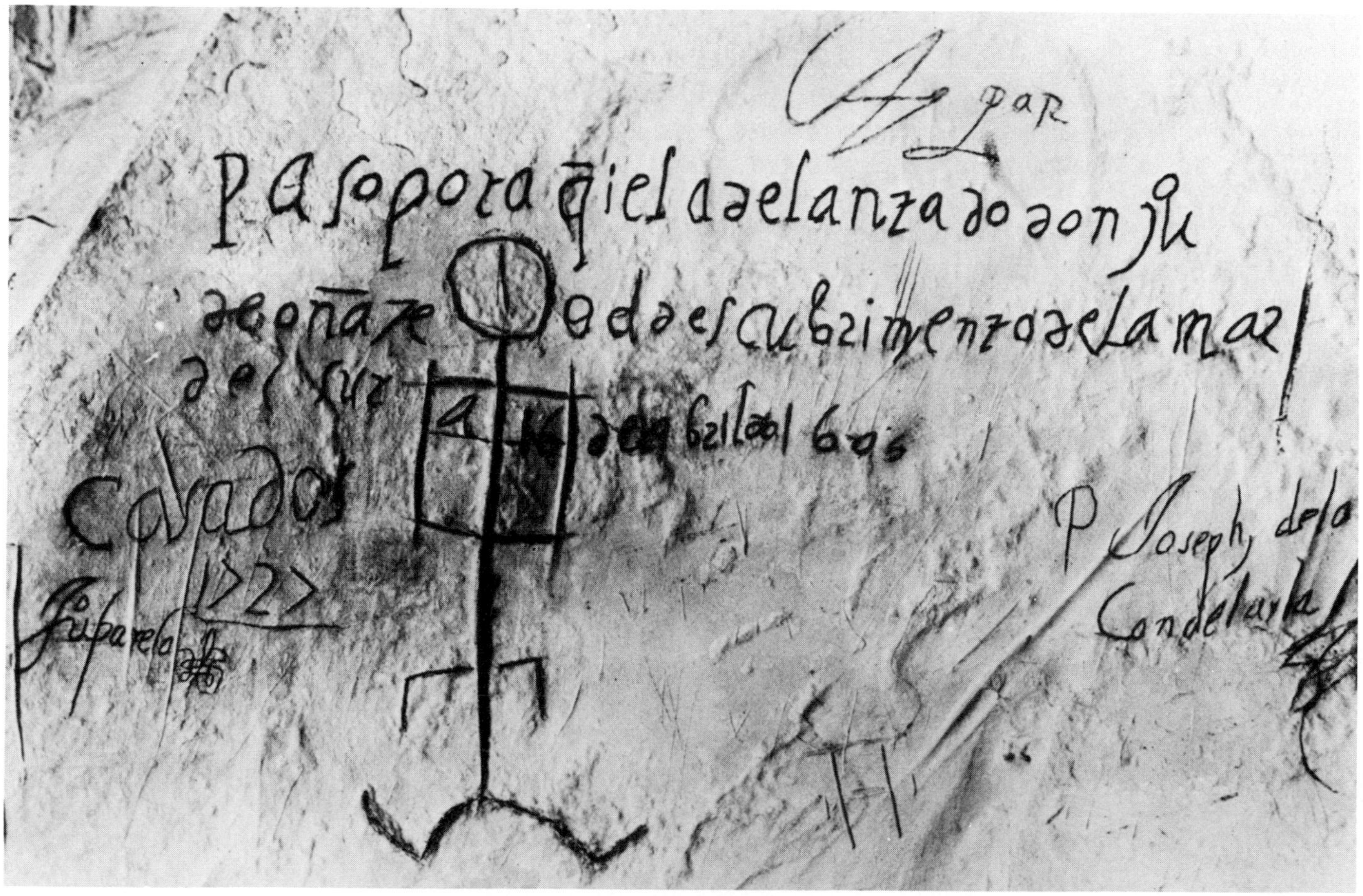

The first serious confrontation between Oñate's men and the Pueblo Indians took place December 4, 1598, on Acoma Mesa. After feigning friendship the natives attacked a Spanish foraging party that had climbed up to the village to secure supplies. Eleven soldiers were killed. Others survived by leaping off the mesa to the plain 400 feet below. Six weeks later the Spaniards retaliated, capturing and burning the pueblo and taking over 500 captives. MNM (#68736)

doned. Thus a new governor was appointed, although to a colony that had changed its nature. Instead of the once-anticipated loads of silver being carried to the homeland, now supply trains to the colony would carry cloth, holy images, nails, and axes for the construction of new missions, largely paid for by the Crown.

In a missionary colony—or at least such was the idea—blue-robed Franciscans would labor patiently at missions in the various pueblos while the civil authorities would govern the Christian population. As soon as the Indians learned Christian and Spanish ways—the two were taken to be synonymous—the region would become a solid member of the Spanish Empire. It did not turn out this way. Instead, the 1600s became what one historian has called "troublous times."

The basic problem was the split between the religious and the governmental sides of Spain's effort. The pile of grey limestone ruins on its lonely hill at almost exactly the center of the state, now the Gran Quivira unit of Salinas National Monument, may be taken as a case study.

The Indian town had been there for centuries before Oñate came riding up the hill. It was one of the fringe pueblos, a go-between for trade between the Rio Grande pueblos and the Plains Indians, as well as the Apaches. Trade items included pottery, corn, and piñon nuts. The nearby salt beds provided a special trade item and also gave the area its common name, the Salinas Province. As in all other pueblos, there was a rich ceremonial year. There was no difference between civil and religious government; all life was bound up in activities that were at once religious and practical. Planting corn was a religious act, and praying a practical one.

And then Oñate and more than 100 men came up the hill. It was an October day in 1598. The colony at San Juan was just two months old, and already Oñate was on the road, visiting the pueblos he anticipated administering. The record says merely that the villages "rendered obedience to His Majesty," but from other instances we know something of the pomp of

Left
For many years Apaches from the East came to Gran Quivira for trade, but the relationship withered. During the 1670s all the Saline pueblos were abandoned because of drought and Apache hostility. Gran Quivira is now part of Salinas National Monument, administered by the National Park Service. NPS

Below
Erected circa 1630 under the direction of Franciscan friars, the Quarai Mission Church served Pueblo Indians living near the salt lakes east of the Manzano Mountains. NMSRCA

the ceremony. The Indians were instructed that these officers and priests now had authority over them. The lesson was driven home in the next year or so as there were two, possibly three, armed conflicts with the newcomers. It is not clear from the record exactly where the fights were, but if not at this town they were nearby and with friends and relatives of these people. The Spanish were bloodily victorious each time, and the new regime settled in.

In 1626 a priest visited the town. Fray Alonso Benavides was a remarkable man, and his report on the missionary potential in New Mexico would do much to bring the colony to the attention of the church. He recorded that he preached a sermon in the plaza and was well received. In 1629 several new priests came northward with the biannual packtrain, and one of them, Fray Francisco Letrado, was assigned to this town. For the first time there was a full-time Spanish presence. Of course Letrado built a church, its ruins a rectangle of fallen walls today. It must have been a lonely and frustrating job. Today one can stand in the remains of his living quarters (his rooms are larger than the Indian rooms) and look out and imagine this devoted man, impossibly distant from home and relatives, laboring against the blank wall of a totally different conception of religion, God, and man. There only a short time, Letrado was transferred to Acoma, where on February 22, 1632 (a century to the day before an English child was born in another colony on the other side of the continent and christened George Washington), he was killed by the Indians.

Priests were few and far between in New Mexico, and it was a generation before Fray Letrado was replaced. The church he built fell into ruin; archeologists find that beams from it were used to repair Indian rooms. There were active churches at the pueblos just a day's walk away, though, and in many ways life was affected by Spaniards, even if they were not always present. Indians had to walk to Santa Fe to work in the governor's sweatshops, their fields suffering in their absence. They had to gather salt and lug it in leather sacks over to the Rio Grande, to meet the mule trains that took it south to the mining towns in Parral. There were also demands from the Spaniards for piñon nuts, for cotton mantas. The Indians, whom the priests saw as a mission field, were actually turning out to be the economic base for the colony.

Eventually, in 1660, another priest came. His name was Fray Diego de Santander, and, inevitably, he wanted to build another church. This one would be huge, its fort-like stone walls up to six feet thick, with attached workshops, classrooms, priest's quarters, storerooms, and a corral. The labor, of course, was immense.

Records do not give us the day-to-day details, but there must have been good times, years when the crops were adequate. There were classes for the children, and there was fascination in the mysteries of the candle-light church. But overall, the story was one of disintegration. Throughout the colony the schism between church and state burst wide open, much of it over control of the Indians. There were a few governors who supported the church, but in the main the governors were out to make what they could during their limited term of office, and that meant using Indian labor. But the church, too, made de-

The Palace of the Governors, constructed soon after the founding of Santa Fe in 1610, is the oldest public building in the United States. The adobe structure served as both residence and executive offices for New Mexico's governors under Spanish, Mexican, and United States administrations. Today it contains exhibits of the Museum of New Mexico. NMSRCA

Because of its strategic location in a natural pass between the Rio Grande and the eastern plains, the pueblo of Abó was an important trade center in prehistoric times. Like their neighbors at Gran Quivira, Abó's people belonged to the Tompiro linguistic group. Franciscan missionaries built San Gregorio church beside the pueblo early in the seventeenth century. NPS

mands on the Indians, to tend fields and herds, to gather firewood, to cook.

As for things of the spirit, there was absolute turmoil. Priests demanded that the kiva ceremonies stop and occasionally went so far as to destroy kivas and their paraphenalia; at the same time there were government officials who at least condoned and sometimes even encouraged the dancers. Whom were the Indians to believe? Word spread like wildfire of the time in the church at Quarai that the *alcalde mayor* stood up during the sermon and disputed the priest, who had just said the Indians owed their allegiance to God. The alcalde said no, they owed their allegience to the governor. After several such incidents, the church brought in the Inquisition, a formidable weapon against its enemies. (A friend to historians, though: Inquisition charges brought against anyone, especially a governor, led to testimony, of which Inquisition officials kept meticulous records. Those fragile pages are the source of much of this story.)

Worse still, relations with the Indians' old trading partners, the Apaches, began to break down, at least in part because the Spaniards occasionally captured Apaches and sold them south into man-killing slavery in the silver mines. The Apaches saw that the Spaniards were living with the Pueblos, and, on the theory that "the friend of my enemy is my enemy," began attacking the pueblos. The situation was exacerbated by a drought in the 1660s that would not let up. There had been droughts before, of course, but never under these circumstances. The age-old pueblo ceremonies to make nature do as it ought had been disrupted, so there was no particular reason for the Indians to think it would get better. The Apaches, suffering themselves from the drought, burned fields and stole stored grain. Drought brought starvation; the *alcalde mayor* of the Salinas Province wrote that when his men went to collect corn from the Indians, "they weep and cry out as if they and all their descendants were being killed." (They were.) And disease came riding on the back of starvation.

The source of their troubles was not lost on the Indians. In the late 1660s Indian leader Esteban Clemente rose in the Salinas Province and attempted to organize a

Acoma's original village was situated high atop a steep-sided mesa for defensive purposes. The location made water a precious commodity. Today the old pueblo is still occupied, but most tribal members live in new communities on the flatlands below. From the D. Woodward Collection, NMSRCA

revolt. He was found out and hanged. But the troubles proved too much; by 1676 the hill at Gran Quivira was abandoned by Pueblo and Spaniard alike.

This was Gran Quivira but it could have been Pecos, or Acoma, or the Galisteo pueblos, or any of a dozen others. In this case the pueblo simply fell apart, never to be reoccupied. But others with similar experiences were still occupied, seething with trouble and resentment and about to boil over into the bloody days of August 1680.

There was long preparation for the revolt. Stimulated by hardship and encouraged by signs of Spanish disunity, Pueblo leaders met to discuss what to do, and the idea evolved of throwing the Spaniards out, lock, stock, and barrel. It is incredible that this joint planning took place at all, for traditionally the various Indian pueblos were fiercely independent. Even more remarkable, the planning took place without the Spaniards' knowledge. It seems that only days before the revolt, the government—headquartered at Santa Fe since 1610—thought everything was as usual.

One of the organizers of the Pueblo Revolt was a San Juan religious leader known as Popé. In a routine exercise at rooting out the Indians' religion in 1675, Spaniards had flogged a number of Indians at Santa Fe, probably including Popé. His revenge would be terrible.

Popé moved to the remote pueblo of Taos in the final months of preparation. From there the word went out to pueblos as distant as Zuni and Hopi, brought by runners who carried a knotted rope. Each knot represented a day left before the uprising; when the last knot was undone, the revolt would begin.

The Spaniards did receive some warning, but it did them little good. On August 8, 1680, Fray Fernando de

Velasco at Pecos learned from Indians there that an uprising was scheduled for the thirteenth. He wrote to Governor Otermín at the Palace of the Governors in Santa Fe, who received the note the next day, along with similar warnings from Taos and elsewhere, and even from captured messengers at Tesuque. For some reason Otermín did not respond quickly, but in any case he probably would not have been quick enough. Either the Indians changed the day once their plan was discovered, or the thirteenth had been a ruse all along. On Saturday the tenth the revolt came.

Death, revenge, and a terrible form of a people's renewal burst upon the Spaniards from a reservoir that had been filling for eighty years. Priests of the new religion were killed in or near their churches. The churches themselves—all of them—were desecrated. Whole Spanish families were wiped out, save those who could flee to the temporary safety of Santa Fe. There the Palace of the Governors became an armed, wailing camp as the refugees straggled in. All in all, more than 400 Spaniards would be killed in the uprising, including twenty-one friars.

By August 12, Indians surrounded the Palace of the Governors. Word reached Governor Otermín that the Rio Abajo (Lower River) ranches near present-day Albuquerque had been totally wiped out. This story later proved to be false and may even have been told deliberately by the Indians, but it brought home to the besieged Spaniards their isolation. In a dramatic gesture one Indian leader, wearing the sash of a slain priest, offered a red cross or a white one—"peace or war." But there was no possibility of reconciliation, and the battle raged.

There is a church in Santa Fe today called "the oldest church." An image of the Blessed Virgin was kept there, and some brave soul rescued it and brought it through the turmoil to the Palace. Soon the besieged could see the smoke of that building mixing with that of burning houses and shops. The little statue would appear again in the story of New Mexico.

It is remarkable that the Spaniards were able to break out of this seemingly impossible situation. Actually there are indications that once the Spaniards chose to leave, the Indians were willing to let them go. On August 21, about 1,000 survivors,

During the 1680 Pueblo revolt, Spaniards from the Rio Abajo (down-river region) assembled at the pueblo of Isleta before retreating down the Rio Grande. That pueblo's church may be the oldest in New Mexico. Although the church has been remodeled frequently, parts of its current foundation and walls were put up about 1613. From the Cobb Collection. Courtesy, University of New Mexico General Library, Special Collections

During the 1680 revolt, Pecos Indians destroyed the massive mission church that the Franciscans had erected south of their pueblo. After the Vargas reconquest, a smaller church was superimposed on the old foundations. This aerial view shows the remains of that church and adjoining convento, *following National Park Service stabilization. NPS*

many of them now widowed or orphaned, made their way out of Santa Fe and started downriver.

Santo Domingo . . . San Felipe . . . at one settlement after another their worst fears were realized. Bodies lay motionless in the sun, the charred remains of buildings behind them. Somewhere along the way Otermín learned that, although the revolt had indeed included the Rio Abajo, there had been survivors who even now were fleeing southward, in the belief that all those at Santa Fe had perished. He sent word for them to wait and caught up at the campsite of Fray Cristóbal. Together the ragged, grieving crowd of 2,500 trudged south to El Paso, where at last they felt out of reach of the terror. The first attempt at European colonization of New Mexico had been extinguished.

Far to the north, there was rejoicing. The images in the churches were destroyed, as were many of the buildings themselves. The great church at Pecos, largest in New Mexico until the modern age, went up in a huge blaze, and its burned adobe blocks reappeared in brand-new kivas. The Palace of the Governors was divided into the small Indian rooms that characterized a traditional pueblo. The old kachina dances were performed again and again, celebrating freedom and the chance to renew old ways. It was an orgy of purification.

It was twelve years before the Spaniards came back, but the celebrating did not last that long. With Spanish repression removed, the alliance quickly collapsed, and age-old rivalries reasserted themselves. Soon there was warfare between the recent allies, and the Apaches and Utes began raiding again.

Of course the Spaniards were not completely forgotten. From year to year there were probes from the south, as Otermín and others made various attempts to reconquer the lost territory. In some ways it is curious that the authorities in Mexico City kept trying, for the colony never had returned much. But the world scene was changing, and Spain was losing its monopoly in the New World. France especially was a threat, with its growing presence in the eastern part of North America. Even if New Mexico could never deliver the riches once imagined, it could serve as a buffer to keep France from approaching the heartland of New Spain.

RECONQUEST

It was dark inside the wrappings. La Conquistadora, the small statue of the Virgin that had been rescued and taken south during the Pueblo Revolt, was now carefully wrapped and being carried in a jolting, screeching oxcart, approaching Santa Fe once again. The Spaniards were back.

Bringing La Conquistadora was the reconquerer who would eventually succeed at the job, with the formidable name Diego José de Vargas Zapata y Lujan Ponce de León y Contreras, commonly referred to as Diego de Vargas. Vargas had gathered 300 men at El Paso, and in August of 1692—twelve years and one week after the first terrible day of the revolt—set out to see if reconquest was possible. The way was hard, and caution was the watchword, for the few previous tentative probes had found the Indians still implacable. Still, 300 men is a significant force. They reached the north country to find pueblos recently abandoned, with crops near harvest. Santo Domingo was empty, as was Cochití. It was obvious that the Indians had fled to the hills and were watching the invaders from there.

Vargas' force approached Santa Fe. Of course the Indians knew they were coming, but what would the reception be? Before dawn on September 13, the tense army gathered silently in a broken-down rancho a few miles from Santa Fe. (It had once belonged to Roque Madrid, Vargas' *maestre de campo,* who must have had memories that night.) The attempt to retake Santa Fe was to be peaceful if possible, but swords were sharpened and ready.

The next day the Indians were defiant. They gathered on the walls of the palace and shouted at the Spaniards assembled before them. But Vargas quickly demonstrated the remarkable courage and restraint that were to serve him so well. Seeing the acequia, the irrigation ditch that supplied water to the city, he cut it off—as the Indians had done in 1680—and boldly walked into Santa Fe with an assumption of victory. The defiance withered, and Vargas won without a fight.

Standing high on a hill overlooking Santa Fe, the Cross of the Martyrs was erected in 1920 by the Knights of Columbus and the Historical Society of New Mexico as a memorial to the Franciscan friars killed during the Pueblo Revolt of 1680. After the neighborhood around the cross became heavily populated, civic groups put up a second cross on a nearby hill for use during ceremonial processions. MNM (#52461)

At Pecos the Indians abandoned the pueblo and fled to the hills; Vargas captured several and, after five days, released them with messages of peace. Vargas then left without damaging the pueblo or stealing its stores. It was a critical decision, for the Pecos would become the Spaniards' most important allies in the difficult decade to come.

The pattern would repeat itself throughout New Mexico. Tesuque . . . San Ildefonso . . . Picurís . . . at pueblo after pueblo Vargas arrived with restrained but obvious force, and with nervous relief the Indians capitulated. Undoubtedly there was something of a domino effect at work, for each pueblo had heard that the pueblo

After the successful recapture of Santa Fe from Pueblo Indian rebels late in 1693, victorious Spanish soldiers attributed their success to a small statue of Our Lady of the Rosary, which they had brought back after a long exile near present El Paso. The image soon became known as "La Conquistadora." Photo by Robert Martin, MNM (#41984)

before had accepted this Spaniard, which made it easier for them also to do so. Time and time again the soldiers heard "the speech," reclaiming the land and all its people in the name of King Carlos II. Priests were kept busy baptizing children born since the revolt and blessing marriages which had taken place. The army marched through the snow to Taos, and even that powerful pueblo, once headquarters for the revolt, came to cheer the speech and accept the baptism. They promised to keep peace with their neighbors, and warned Vargas of opposition in some of the western pueblos.

Vargas then headed south. He revisited Pecos; this time the Indians welcomed him with boughs and crosses and pledges of allegiance. He visited Santo Domingo and Cochití and was warned of trouble to come at Jemez. It was true, but there, too, his courage and will prevailed without bloodshed.

Now Vargas determined to push on to the western pueblos. He sent part of the army and much of the baggage to wait for him at El Paso, and headed west with a select force. They approached the virtually impregnable mesa at Acoma. Again the general bargained, waited, and chose the precise moment to seize a bloodless victory. The record was unbroken, and when the army stopped at El Morro for water a few days later, Vargas added another message, still visible today, to New Mexico's rock of history: "Here was General Don Diego de Vargas, who conquered all New Mexico for our holy faith and the royal crown at his own expense, the year 1692."

The Hopi mesas brought the greatest danger and the highest drama of the 1692 expedition. Yet even there, facing a seemingly implacable foe, Vargas somehow prevailed by sheer force of personality. Natives who had him vastly outpowered ultimately submitted without a fight and, on bended knee, received "the Reconqueror."

Vargas wasted no time preparing to build on the foundation he had won. Returning to El Paso amid great rejoicing, he once again spent day after day on horseback, this time going from village to village persuading ranchers and miners to join him in settling the land he had reconquered. Although he had hoped for 500 families, he succeeded in enlisting only seventy. Still, by October 1693 he was ready to head north again, this time leading settlers, Indians, herds of cattle and horses, and 100 soldiers to man the presidio in Santa Fe. From now on the seemingly easy glory of reconquest was going to become the hard work of settlement.

His second trek north was cold and difficult. There were rumors that the Pueblo Indians were reverting to their old animosity. When the settlers finally arrived at Santa Fe, they were locked out; the stymied colony camped in the snow outside.

Vargas wished to avoid armed conflict, but this time he could not. Twenty-two Spaniards died of exposure during the snowy wait, while negotiations and mutual insults dragged on. On December 29, 1693, the Spaniards attacked. After a two-day-long battle, the victorious Spaniards executed seventy Indians and enslaved about 400 more for a time. Those who escaped fled through the snow to the outlying pueblos and spread the word: the Spaniards were back.

Four pueblos, most importantly Pecos, cast their lot with the Spaniards, but the rest remained in rebellion. Their stronghold was Black Mesa, behind San Ildefonso. Vargas spent much of 1694 trying to subdue the Indians who held out there, and eventually, by destroying their fields, he succeeded. (Ironically he organized his Pueblo allies with a knotted rope—the same means the Indians had used in the Pueblo Revolt of 1680.) Even then the Spanish hold on New Mexico was tenuous, and in 1696 the northern pueblos revolted again. The outburst was sudden, bloody, and frightening—but Vargas was no Otermín. He and his troops were constantly in the saddle reasserting Spanish dominion. It proved to be the last organized, massive Indian resistance and the beginning of a new era, when the sons and daughters of Spain would sink permanent roots into New Mexico's parched, rocky soil.

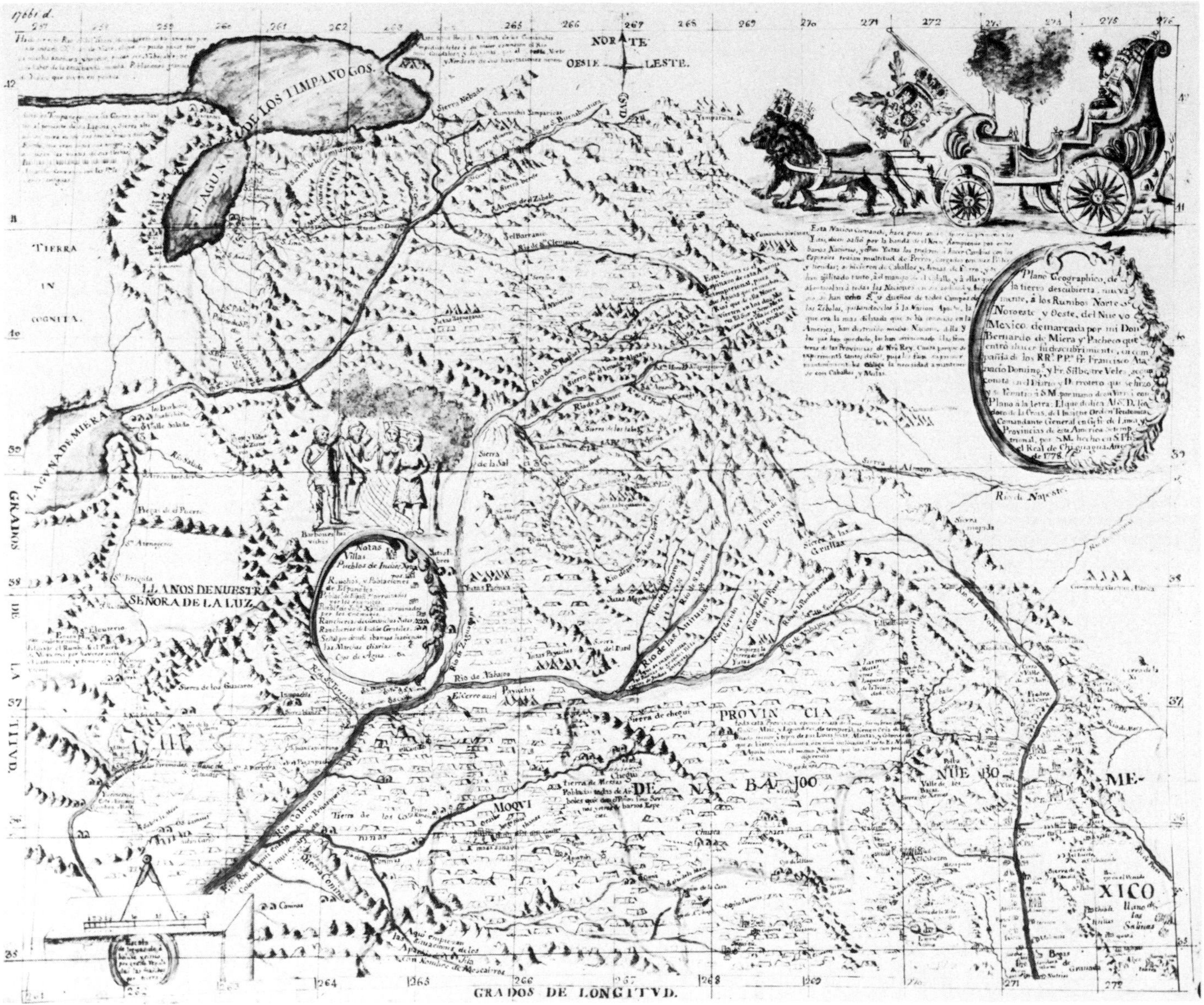

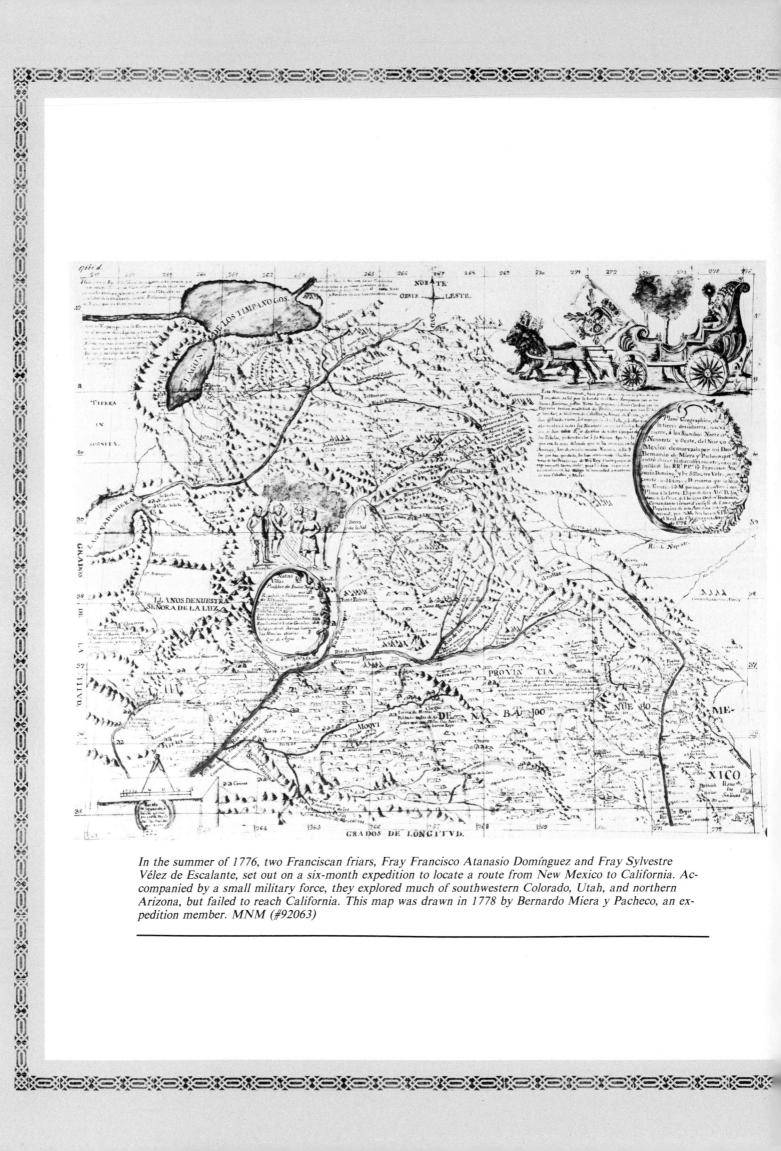

In the summer of 1776, two Franciscan friars, Fray Francisco Atanasio Domínguez and Fray Sylvestre Vélez de Escalante, set out on a six-month expedition to locate a route from New Mexico to California. Accompanied by a small military force, they explored much of southwestern Colorado, Utah, and northern Arizona, but failed to reach California. This map was drawn in 1778 by Bernardo Miera y Pacheco, an expedition member. MNM (#92063)

Spanish Colony, Mexican Territory

History spends much of its time looking at great events, at pivotal points where one force takes over from another. In this light the 1700s were calm, almost static in New Mexico. The century began with the reconquest, and at the end of the century Spain was still in control. Changes were slow and incremental; the 1700s do not get much space in New Mexico history books. In some ways, the history of the state was being written far away on the east coast, where some rambunctious colonies of England revolted and formed a new nation . . . but those were just distant rumors in New Mexico.

Of course, to the people living in this "quiet" century—one where not one nation managed to seize power from another—the century did not seem quiet at all. It was a difficult time, filled with hard work and considerable danger. In the previous century the Spanish economy had been built on the backs of the Pueblo Indians by demands for tribute and labor—and that had led to the Pueblo Revolt of 1680. Now Spain was to build a colony that lived on its own labor from the land. That it succeeded at all is a measure of the will of the people who did it, for New Mexico has never been an easy place to make a living.

They began along the river, of course, where there was water and soil for farming. Some of the best land was along the middle Rio Grande, and in 1706 Governor Francisco Cuervo y Valdes formally established a new villa there. Possibly seeking royal favor—his appointment replacing the great Vargas was provisional, pending confirmation—he named it for the viceroy in Mexico, the Duke of Alburquerque (the extra "r" has since been dropped). There were broad, well-watered lands along the river, and Tijeras Pass offered a route through the mountains to the plains. One day the tiny farming village would become a great center of the Southwest.

Naturally, these parcels so desirable to the Spanish colonial farmers had not gone unnoticed by Pueblo Indian farmers, and competition was inevitable. In theory, the king owned all the land and could grant it to whomever he chose. This radical position was tempered, though, by a quite genuine belief in the rights of Indians, and various Pueblos retained the areas they had long inhabited. There were numerous court cases involving Spaniards accused of trespassing on Indian lands, and often enough the Indians won. Mutual infringements took many forms. Some irrigation systems were operated jointly by Indians and Spaniards, with resulting conflicts over who was to make repairs and who got first crack at the water. Cattle wandering onto fields were a continuing sore point, as were "unused" grounds owned by one party but desired by another.

As Spanish children reached maturity, the limited farmlands became inadequate. The normal solution was to petition the governor for new land grants. One such case can stand for many. In 1751 twelve families petitioned the governor for land where they would found a new settlement, in a small, well-watered valley in the Sangre de Cristos high above Santa Fe. The petition was researched: did anyone

C H A P T E R V

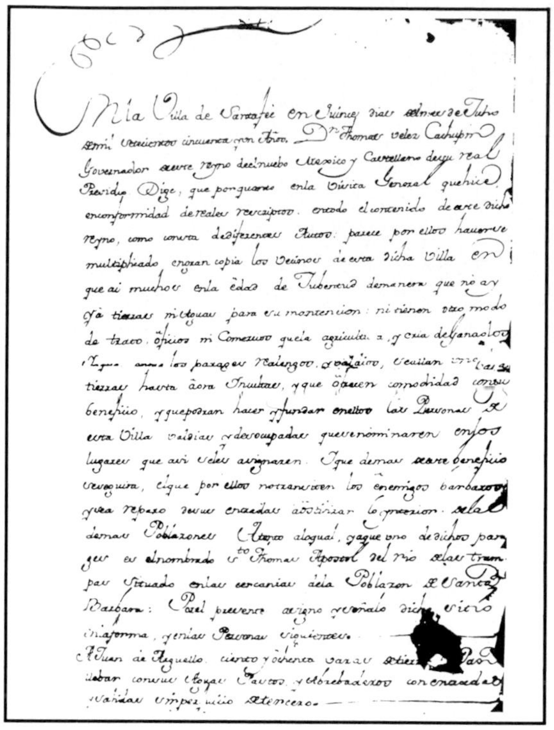

On July 15, 1751, Don Tomás Vélez Cachupín, governor of New Mexico and commander of the Santa Fe presidio, approved a request made by twelve families for a land grant at Las Trampas. The settlers were given the tract in an ancient ritual conducted by the alcalde mayor, *a leading local official. From the Spanish Archives of New Mexico, NMSRCA*

else want the land? Was there a prior grant? (The Spanish bureaucracy was meticulously legal.) In this case the petition was granted. The alcalde accompanied the settlers to the valley that would be their new home. He showed them the boundaries which had been set out by the governor, after which they repeated the medieval ritual of pulling up grass and throwing rocks within the boundaries they had been granted. The tiny village of San José de Gracias de Las Trampas came into being.

In accordance with frontier policy, the village was laid out for defense, with the houses and church fronting on an enclosed square, presenting blank, defensible walls to the outside. An acequia from a point on the stream somewhat higher in the valley was brought down the side of the valley. From it water could be channeled into fields, which were long and narrow so that each field could touch the acequia. They built their church with adobe from a nearby hillside, cleared fields, raised children. In 1776, as an unheard war raged on the other side of a continent, there were 278 people in Las Trampas. There were good years, when the rains came and the frosts stayed away, when children were raised in health; but there were disastrous years too, of crop failure, of Indian raids, and the terrible time in the 1780s when smallpox swept the valley. All this and more came to be part of the village memory.

In 1982 this writer spent some time helping plaster the church in Las Trampas. It was worth four or five history courses to hear the worn, strong-spirited people who live there talk of the village. A dog's bark across the valley is easily heard, and a pickup truck intrudes only rarely. When we went to a hillside to get dirt for adobe, they explained that this was where their fathers had dug it the first time—in 1760—and they still got it there "so the color would be the same." But perhaps it was too easy to be carried away with the peace of those autumn days. The people also talked of the disaster of unemployment, of men injured in the mines a few miles away, and of the difficulties of hauling timber in winter.

In spite of competition in the fields and in the courts, Pueblo and Spaniard drew together to ward off danger from new directions. The Apaches, who had begun their rise the previous century, continued it with a vengeance; and the Navajos to the west and northwest saw rich pickings in the isolated Spanish and Pueblo settlements, especially as they gained arms and horses from the Spaniards. Utes appeared in the north, and Comanches began riding in from the plains to the east. Isolated villages were in almost constant danger, and Pueblos just a generation after the revolt found themselves garnering praise as effective military auxiliaries during Spanish counterraids. Scattered ranches and settlements, like Las Trampas, often suffered small, sudden, violent raids. Sometimes they were conducted on a large scale. In 1760 Comanches attacked a hacienda near Taos and killed at least fourteen, taking many others prisoner. In 1775 it was Comanches again who attacked the Pueblo of Sandia and drove off the horses, then trapped and killed the thirty-two Pueblo men who pursued them. Two years later Apaches attacked Valencia and killed twenty-three settlers. Albuquerque itself

lost citizens to occasional raids and, once, its whole *remuda* (string of horses). The ordinary response was for community leaders to pursue the raiders, almost always without result. Against such hit-and-run tactics the soldiers of the presidio and their Pueblo auxiliaries could hardly be effective.

The constant exchange between Spaniard and Indian, sometimes military and sometimes trading, gave rise to a class of people unique to New Mexico. *Genízaros,* they were and are called, Indians by race but Spanish by culture. Many Indian children were captured or bartered for, and ended up in the Spanish settlements. Others simply wandered in. Never quite accepted as Spaniards, they became neither Indian nor fully Spanish. They secured land grants, settled in villages of their own—Abiquiu north of Santa Fe is one—and played a major role in the colony. One historian has estimated that by the late 1700s they were one-third of the population.

In 1779 Don Juan Bautista de Anza, one of New Mexico's greatest governors, took the war to the Comanches' doorstep

Far Left
Far from urban centers where it could be bought, New Mexicans began to make their own religious art. Part of the Museum of New Mexico collection, this representation of San Rafael is the work of Don Bernardo Miera y Pacheco, an important eighteenth-century cartographer who accompanied the Domínguez-Escalante expedition in 1776. SHPB

Below
Las Trampas still retains the feeling of an eighteenth-century village. At that time Spanish governmental regulations required that frontier settlements be laid out around a central plaza for defense. MNM (#11561)

in eastern Colorado. The Comanches were utterly surprised and defeated, and Anza forced a treaty that was respected by both sides for generations. But attacks continued from other quarters. In fact, the problem would last another century, through another government entirely, and on into a third.

Remarkably, hostilities were generally suspended for the annual Indian trade fairs, a tradition of long standing, as Indians from the plains met at Pecos, Taos, or Abiquiu to trade for the goods of the Rio Grande pueblos. The Spaniards participated in these but had their own trading adventure as well: the caravan to Mexico City or, by the mid-1700s, Chihuahua. A half-dozen or so New Mexico merchants assembled at the point and time announced by the governor to form the annual caravan. Then settlers from villages and ranches joined with items to take south, to be traded for products not available on the remote frontier. They brought a few crops but also tanned hides, wool, piñon nuts, and salt from the salt lakes near present-day Estancia. Pretty soon the long, dusty caravan moved, often escorted by some ragged soldiers from the presidio in Santa Fe. It is the regret of every New Mexico historian that no diaries of members of the annual caravans have surfaced. We know the caravans made their way downriver past present-day Socorro, struggled across the Jornada del Muerto, and rested briefly at El Paso. There they picked up a few more merchants with barrels of "Pass wine" and continued on across the terrible sand dunes of the Medanos and down the long, hard trail to Chihuahua. The dust of the approaching caravan sent prices skyrocketing, and a complex system of coinage and exchange rates guaranteed that no northerner was going to come out ahead of the game.

Of course the New Mexico traders knew what was happening—their empty purses told them—but they were between the rock of necessity and the hard place of Spanish policy. The policy ruled that Spanish colonies must trade only with Spanish colonies or the motherland. There were two very different views of the northern colony. For those living in it, it was home, where one worked to stay warm, to have food, to raise a family, and to live the good life. For those of this view, the merchant who appeared unexpectedly from the east, speaking perhaps French but selling his wares at a good price, was a godsend. (In 1739 just this happened, when the Mallet brothers appeared with trade goods. It was not the last time.) But in the view from Mexico City, New Mexico was the first line of defense in a game of global politics. Spain had been first into the New World, and her glorious empire was not without competitors. England and France had established themselves on the eastern half of the northern landmass and were obviously not content to stay there. Struggles in the Old World were reflected in the new, and the prairies were proving too porous a barrier. Like those houses in remote, threatened villages, New Mexico could present her doors to the motherland, her blank walls to everyone else. Travel was strictly regulated in New Mexico. When a caravan or group of traders came through town, the *alcalde mayor* was re-

Left
During the eighteenth century most New Mexicans were subsistence farmers whose patron saint was San Isidro Labrador. Carved by José Benito Ortega, a santero *from Mora, this image is displayed at the Museum of New Mexico. According to tradition, the angel assures that San Isidro receives divine assistance. SHPB*

Opposite, top
Described by one authority as "the most perfectly-preserved Spanish Colonial church in the United States," the Church of San José de Gracia was built in the 1760s at Las Trampas, a mountain village thirty-five miles south of Taos. SHPB

Opposite, bottom
Although Spanish settlers and their northern Ute neighbors fought, they traded actively between skirmishes. The deerskins that the settlers obtained from the Utes and other tribes were among the few items for which there was a demand in Chihuahua and other commercial centers to the south. From the McNitt Collection, NMSRCA

quired to notify the governor of all who were in it. A permit was required to travel almost anywhere. By wading through the mountain of paperwork that continually came into his office, the governor was immediately aware of any newcomers in the territory and anyone heading toward the border. Much of this red tape that so overburdened the governor was so that the authorities down in Mexico could keep track of events in New Mexico. Spain was just as worried about French and English traders—and after the revolution, the vigorous entrepreneurs from the fledgling United States—as she was about their soldiers.

Spain had reason to be worried.

In 1806 a small, ragged United States Army exploring party, led by Lieutenant Zebulon Pike, was struggling across the plains. As they approached the Rocky Mountains they either became or pretended to become lost. Historians still debate just what their orders were; lost or not, the group was inevitably following the restless westering of the young United States. The Spaniards sent a force onto the plains to intercept the weathered band. There is something symbolic about those two forces: on one side was the United States, represented by Pike and his eighteen trail-

In late February 1807, a Spanish patrol captured Zebulon M. Pike and his men on Conejos Creek in present southern Colorado. After preliminary questioning in Santa Fe the prisoners were marched to Chihuahua for further interrogation before being allowed to return to the United States. Pike was killed April 27, 1813, during the Battle of York, a significant engagement of the War of 1812 fought near present Toronto. MNM (#7757)

weary men; while on the other was the Spanish Lieutenant don Facundo Melgares and his 600 men, their remuda of over 2,000 horses, according to some sources, carefully selected even for color. How could one know that this powerful force was almost the last gasp of an empire that was losing its three centuries' hold on New Mexico, the small ragged force the first intimation of an empire that was coming? The clue came a little later. The two detachments failed to encounter each other on the plains, but a few months later Pike was desperately bivouacked in the Colorado mountains, caught by winter. Melgares captured—perhaps rescued is a better word—the pitiful force and brought it into Santa Fe. They were trespassers, the old regulations were still in effect, and Melgares was told to take Pike to Chihuahua for the authorities to decide what to do with this international intruder. After a dinner (with plenty of wine, Pike noted) in the venerable mud Palace of the Governors, they left into the snowy night, first in the governor's carriage and then on horseback. They made their way down La Bajada—the steep, rugged hill that for centuries had been a bane to oxcart drivers on the Camino Real—and stopped for the night in the little village at its foot. Melgares went to sleep, while Pike stayed up to talk with the local priest. If ever there was a representative of Old Spain, it is the local frontier priest, but this one's conversation surprised Pike. The priest wanted to know what the United States was like and when they were coming, giving Pike the impression that he, the priest, would be glad when that happened.

The "quiet" century, the 1700s, in which no empire replaced another, was over. People had lived and died, families and villages had been established, and rival empires had learned a little more of the distant land. Perhaps unintentionally, preparations had been made for tremendous change in New Mexico.

Two influences from the United States arrived in New Mexico early in the 1800s. One went around the world and came by way of Spain; the other came straight across the plains in canvas-covered wagons. They met in Santa Fe.

It is too simple to credit the U.S. example alone with igniting the democratic revolutionary fires that burned in so many places in the late 1700s, but the Revolutionary War in the English colonies had been the most successful, and the most obvious, challenge to the old order. Europeans had watched it with fear or envy, depending on their social perspective. After Napoleon's occupation of Spain, in 1810 a government-in-exile instituted changes that were almost democratic. For the first time in memory they called a *"cortes,"* a type of parliament used long before. Orders to elect representatives went across the ocean to New Spain and in a saddlebag up the long, lonely Camino Real to distant New Mexico. A New Mexico representative, Don Pedro Bautista Pino, actually made the trip to Spain to give New Mexico a voice in deliberations

that were called to give Spain a constitution. As it turned out, when circumstances in Europe changed and the monarch was restored, he declared the whole thing had been a mistake. Nevertheless, fires once started are not so easily put out. Revolution—bloody, confused, and stumbling, but still revolution—broke out in New Spain. In September 1821 New Mexico was no longer the most distant outpost of a European-based Spanish Empire; instead it was the most distant outpost of a new country, Mexico.

Most New Mexicans probably never noticed. The various maneuverings of the revolution itself had been but distant rumors, and when finally the revolution was over, it was weeks before the word arrived in Santa Fe. (The governor reported to Mexico City that there was a glorious celebration at the news.) Still, New Mexico was as distant a place as ever. There were irrigation ditches to clean, sheep to shear, the sick to tend, Indian attacks to fear, grasshopper hordes to fight. . . . Distant politics were distant indeed.

The other influence from the United States, the one that came in wagons, was far more immediate. The barrier of the plains had proved porous. The Spaniards had worried about this; in fact, their agent Pedro Vial in his several crossings had shown that practical routes existed. Lieutenant Zebulon Pike's widely circulated report, prepared after his arrest and trip to Mexico, had alerted U.S. merchants to the starved markets in Santa Fe. The payoff, which came after the 1821 Mexican Revolution, was precipitated by a small-time Missouri trader named William Becknell.

It happened that his timing was just right. In the autumn of 1821 Becknell was out on the prairie with a few goods, looking for trade with Indians or whomever else he might encounter on the edges of the forbidden Spanish colony, when a de-

Known as La Bajada (the descent) the rocky escarpment south of Santa Fe has defied travelers for centuries. Although cars and trucks have replaced squeaking carretas *and a modern highway now approximates the historic Camino Real, the hill still challenges motorists on snowy days. From the Virginia Johnson Collection, NMSRCA*

Right
After his ordination as a priest at Durango, Mexico, in 1822 Father Antonio José Martínez became a powerful figure in New Mexico's ecclesiastical and political affairs. He strongly opposed granting large tracts of land to outsiders. In recent years Martínez has evolved into a folk hero for many New Mexicans. MNM (#10308)

tachment of friendly Spanish—no, Mexican—soldiers met him near Raton Pass and invited him in to Santa Fe. There he met the governor, Facundo Melgares, the same man who as a Spanish soldier some fifteen years before had brought Pike in. The message this time was clear and far-reaching: We are now Mexico; we make our own rules; and finally we can trade for your goods. Come on in!

Becknell quickly sold his few goods at a tremendous profit and hurried back to the States. It is said that when he unloaded in Franklin, Missouri, he slashed the leather sack holding his silver profit and let the

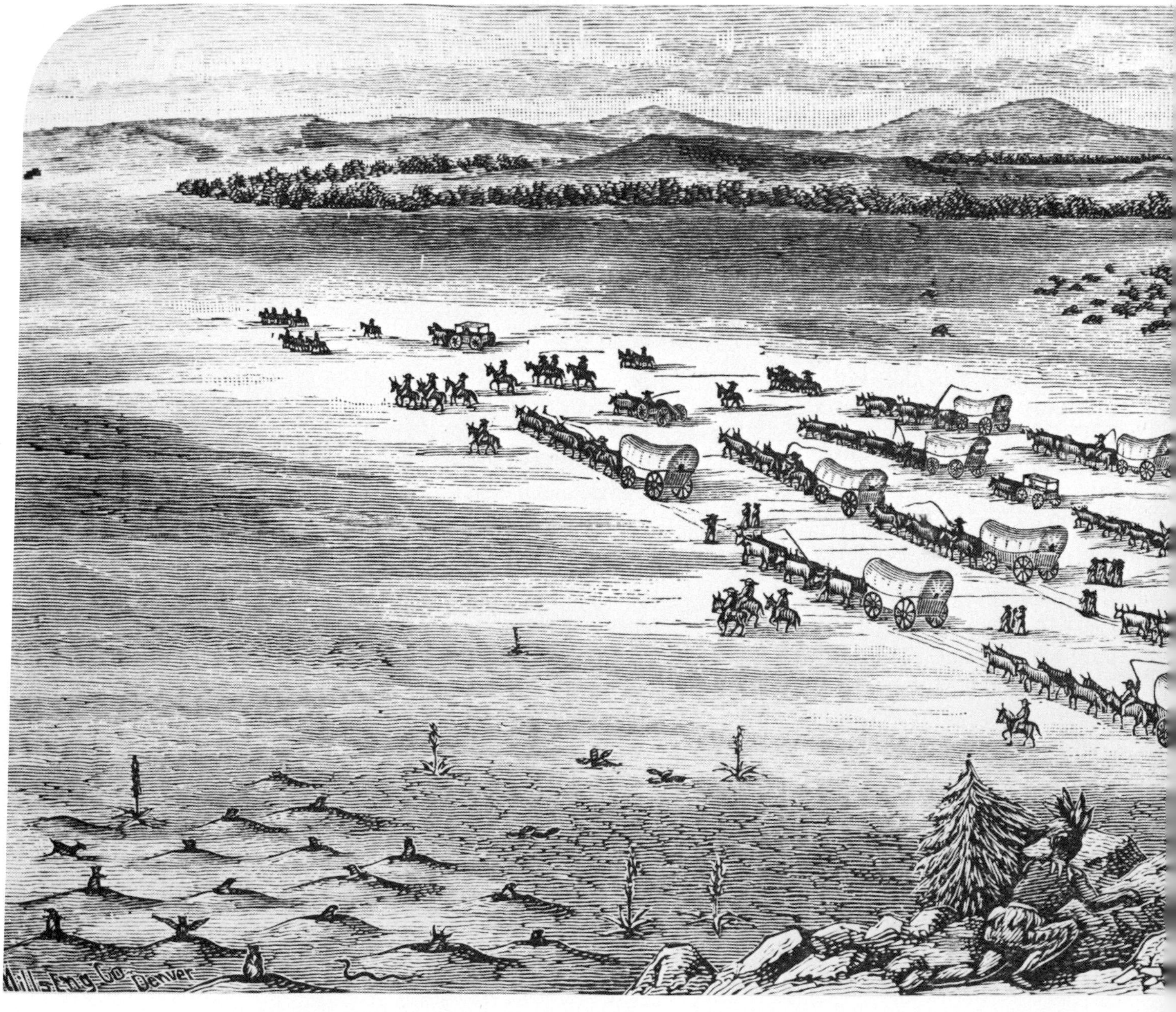

Spanish coins tumble onto the street. It was a dramatic announcement and did not go unnoticed.

Becknell returned in 1822, making two changes that set the pattern for the future. First, he used wagons instead of pack animals, proving they could be manhandled across the prairie. Second, remembering the struggle over Raton Pass, he took a shortcut from the Arkansas River to the Cimarron River to avoid the haul over the pass. It saved 100 miles, but the dry crossing would cost lives before the trail days were over.

The trade grew explosively. Hardscrabble Missouri farmers and storekeepers heard about the profits and jumped on the bandwagon—or rather the Conestoga, virtual symbol of the Santa Fe Trail, whose distinctive sagging bottom and sloped sides kept the cargo stable. Every spring the meadows around the jump-off towns along the Missouri River saw the wagons gather. Many journals and at least one great book, Josiah Gregg's *Commerce of the Prairies,* describe the scene. Each year many men (and animals) were new, and it was chaos. Luckily, the beginning of the route was relatively easy. First-timers copied old-timers in packing the all-important cargo. Cantankerous mules were broken to harness, and routines worked out. By Council Grove, 150 miles out, men knew their jobs, one another, and their animals a little better. They cut hardwood logs for replacement axles (there would be none out on the prairies, they heard around the campfires) and organized for the true crossing, which at that point began.

It is symbolic of American ways that

Bottom, left
Reproduced from an early edition of Gregg's Commerce of the Prairies, *this engraving illustrates a wagon train crossing the plains of the Santa Fe Trail. The expedition is flanked by prairie dogs, buffalo, and watchful Indians. MNM (#87450)*

Bottom, right
Josiah Gregg's Commerce of the Prairies, *first published in 1844, is the definitive account of the Santa Fe trade between Missouri and New Mexico. The book describes Gregg's adventures on the trail between 1831 and 1840. Gregg brought the first printing press to New Mexico in 1834. MNM (#9896)*

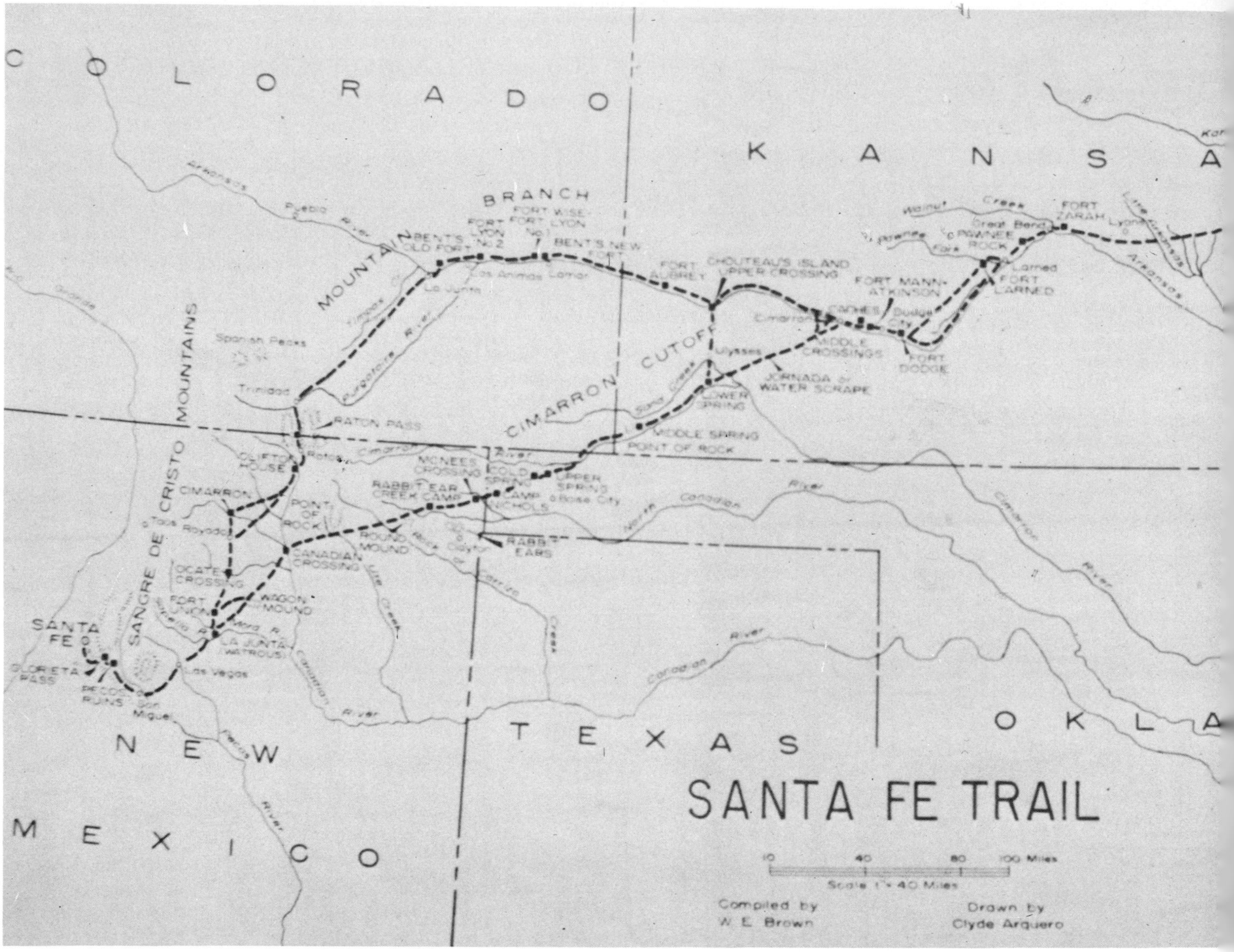

Both the Mountain Branch and the shortcut known as the Cimarron Cutoff are depicted in this map of the Santa Fe Trail. In later years the trail gradually shortened as railroads pushed west and preempted its function. MNM (#45001)

the merchants noisily demanded help from the government, but when the help came it proved unwieldy, so the merchants ignored it anyway. The government decided to map the trail but inexplicably mapped it to Taos; the merchants knew the way and went to Santa Fe. Army escorts for protection from the Indian proved almost useless, so soon the caravans were organized into slowly plodding fortresses.

The Santa Fe Trail was not a single, set trail. If there were no Indians about, the wagons might pull abreast of one another and move across the prairie grass in a broad line, avoiding one another's dust. River crossings, always difficult, might have been best in one place one year, another place the next. Wet weather meant taking the high ground, dry weather dictated a different route. A caravan might have had to go well out of its way to camp near firewood or pasture.

Many a frontiersman, notably Kit Carson who hired onto a Santa Fe wagon train as a runaway, got his first taste of the American West in the Santa Fe trade. The images worked their way into the national folklore. There would be paintings, songs, and legends about the vast prairie, the night sky, campfire talk, Indians on the horizon, and the exhilarating buffalo chase. It was all true, but it wasn't the reason for the trade. The reason was there in the wagons: the flannels and silks and linens, the percussion caps and cooking pots and traps and mirrors, the combs and

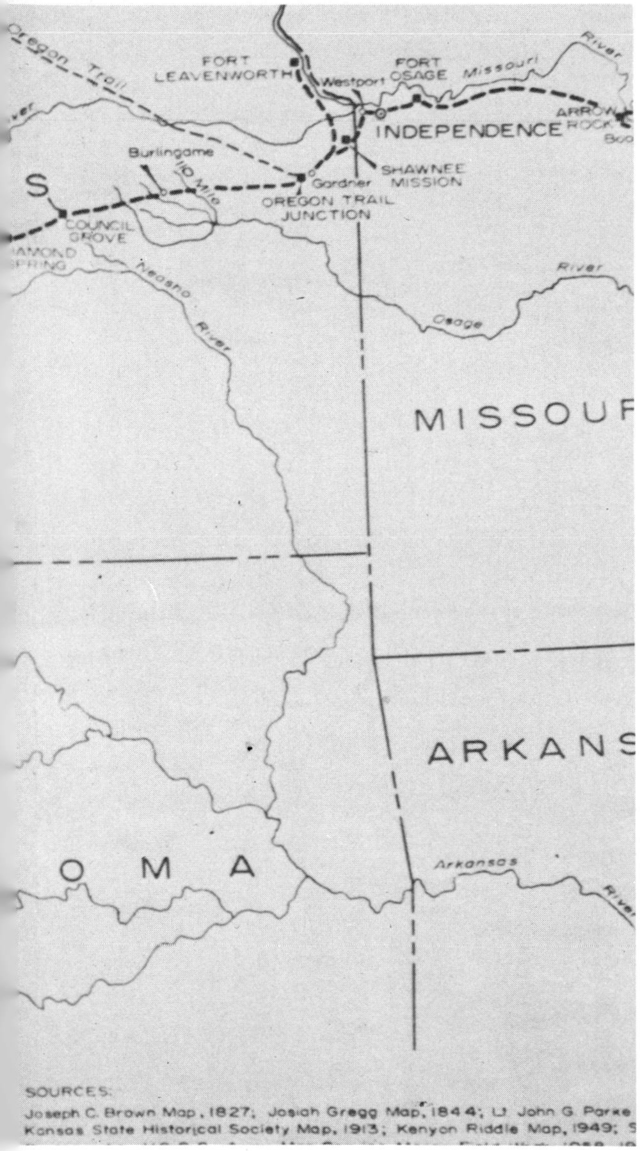

wallpaper and champagne and whiskey. (Traders found they could make a profit even after drinking the latter, so valuable were the bottles to the Indians!)

One day the Sangre de Cristos would be sighted, a thin line on the horizon. The great wagons trudged down the front range, passed the almost-abandoned pueblo of Pecos with its pitiful handful of citizens (soon even they left, and the wagons came past an abandoned ruin, the wagoneers sightseeing, camping in the rooms in bad weather, and stealing souvenirs), and wound through Glorieta Pass. A day out from Santa Fe the traders stopped, shaved, and got out long-saved clean clothes, put new "poppers" on the bullwhips, and came down the long hill into town now called "Old Santa Fe Trail." They had arrived. The hired hands scattered out to the predictable joys of the strange adobe town, while the wagon owners argued, pleaded with, and bribed customs officials, and rented shop space on the plaza. It was time to turn this adventure into profit.

New Mexico certainly needed goods, but this was a flood; in just a few years the New Mexico market was glutted. Still, there was Mexico, just a little further walk. The Santa Fe Trail connected with the centuries-older Camino Real, and soon the wagons were not even unloading in Santa Fe, but continuing on down to Chihuahua. The Chihuahua merchants found that the game had been turned around.

What went back to the States? Silver, some gold (after it was discovered in the Ortiz Mountains southeast of Santa Fe in 1828, setting off a minor rush), furs, and mules. The wagons were not needed for the return trip, so even they were sold for a profit, converted into more silver and mules. Thus Missouri became a hard silver state and gained the long-eared state symbol that lasts to this day. There were other exchanges, too. Traders learned some Spanish, and New Mexicans learned some English. Spanish surnames began showing up on the rolls of finishing schools in St. Louis. If New Mexico under Spain had

Ceran St. Vrain, a leading trader on the Santa Fe Trail, first came to New Mexico in 1825. Six years later he formed a partnership with Charles Bent, which resulted in the construction of Bent's Fort on the Arkansas River. In 1847 Bent was murdered at Taos while serving as New Mexico's first governor after the United States conquest. To avenge his partner's death, St. Vrain enlisted a company of mountain men in Santa Fe who marched north to chastise the rebels. From the Department of Development Collection, NMSRCA

When trade over the Santa Fe Trail was at its peak, merchants often filled the plaza with heavily-laden Conestoga wagons drawn by teams of mules or oxen. Because Mexican authorities sometimes levied import duties on each wagon, the traders piled their goods into enormous loads before entering the city. MNM (#11254)

been an adobe fortress with its blank wall toward the outside world, that wall now had windows in it, and almost a door.

New Mexico under Mexico was changing, and not just by what the wagons were bringing across the prairie. Mexico never did get a firm grip on the colony. The government in Mexico City changed almost monthly; instructions to the colony were slow and confusing; and actual help almost never came up the long road from Mexico City. Spain, having learned that giving an annual gift to the nomadic Indians was much cheaper than fighting them, had worked out a pretty reliable system to see that the necessary funds reached New Mexico. These funds dried up under Mexico. The raids began again, as bad as they ever had been.

The colony the Indians were attacking was not quite sure of its own identity. Age-old ties to Spain had been broken, and ties to an independent Mexico were only tissue. More and more Anglos were coming and staying, marrying into New Mexican families and establishing businesses.

In 1837 taxes were instituted to replace the lost financial support from Mexico. This outraged many New Mexicans, especially the poor in the north. The new governor, Albino Pérez, was not born here, they cried (he was from Mexico, not born in New Mexico). Why should he—this outsider—now levy taxes? From the discontent came another revolt. Governor Pérez and several of his officials were killed, and the rebels entered Santa Fe on August 10, 1837—ironically the very day of the Pueblo Revolt of 1680. But this re-

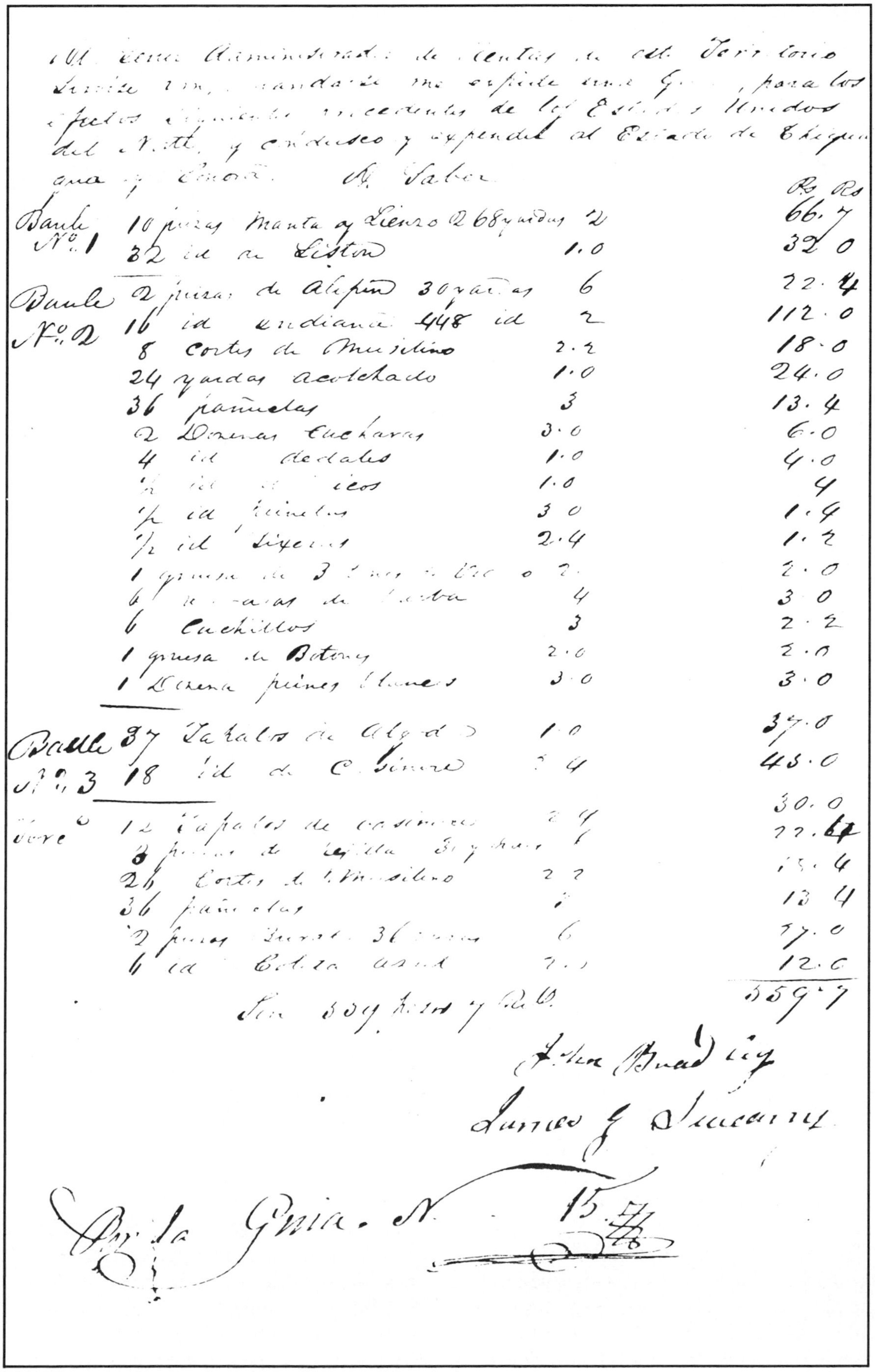

M. [illegible] Administrador de Rentas de este Territorio [illegible] mandar se me expida una Guía para los efectos siguientes procedentes de los Estados Unidos del Norte y conducirlos y expenderlos al Estado de Chihuahua y Sonora. A Saber

			Ps Rs
Baule No. 1	10 piezas Manta y Lienzo 268 yardas	2	66.7
	32 id de Liston	1.0	32.0
Baule No. 2	2 piezas de Alepin 30 yardas	6	22.4
	16 id Indiana 448 id	2	112.0
	8 Cortes de Muselino	2.2	18.0
	24 yardas acolchado	1.0	24.0
	36 pañuelas	3	13.4
	2 Docenas Cucharas	3.0	6.0
	4 id dedales	1.0	4.0
	½ id [illegible]	1.0	4
	½ id peinetas	3.0	1.4
	½ id tijeras	2.4	1.2
	1 gruesa de [illegible]	[illegible]	2.0
	6 [illegible]	4	3.0
	6 Cuchillos	3	2.2
	1 gruesa de Botones	2.0	2.0
	1 Docena peines [illegible]	3.0	3.0
Baule No. 3	37 Tapalos de Algodon	1.0	37.0
	18 id de [illegible]	[illegible]	45.0
			30.0
Sobre	12 Tapalos de [illegible]	[illegible]	22.6
	3 piezas de [illegible]	[illegible]	[illegible]
	26 Cortes de Muselino	2.2	[illegible]
	36 pañuelas	[illegible]	13.4
	2 piezas [illegible] 36 [illegible]	6	27.0
	6 id [illegible]	[illegible]	12.0
	Son 559 pesos y 7 Rs.		559.7

John Bradley

James G. Sweeney

Por la Guía N. 15

Under Mexican law, traders were required to obtain a guía (commercial passport) at Santa Fe before transporting goods down the trail for sale in the interior states. In this example John Bradley and James G. Sweeney requested a license to carry merchandise valued at 559 pesos and seven reales to Chihuahua and Sonora. Their invoice included ribbon, buttons, thimbles, scissors, knives, razors, and spoons. From the Mexican Archives of New Mexico, NMSRCA

Angered by governmental reorganization and a new tax plan, revolutionists from Northern New Mexico assassinated Mexican Governor Albino Pérez on August 9, 1837, during a short-lived rebellion. In 1903 the Daughters of the American Revolution put up this commemorative monument. NMSRCA

volt was neither so organized nor so successful as that long-ago one had been. Manuel Armijo, a merchant with land holdings near Albuquerque and Socorro and one of the remarkable characters of New Mexico history, led an army to Santa Fe to put down the rebellion. The pretender governor was killed, and Armijo assumed the governorship.

Texas, another northern colony which also had the experience of being Spanish one day and vaguely Mexican the next, had a similar revolt, but it was successful. Anglo-Americans had filtered into Texas in such numbers that the colony was almost a U.S. territory. (The first illegal crossings of the river border between the U.S. and Mexico were not south to north, but in the opposite direction.) When Texas succeeded in pulling away from Mexico in 1836, the rebels confidently expected to become part of the United States. The slavery question interfered, and Texas was left as a republic, looking greedily at the weak New Mexican colony to the west. In 1841 Texans invaded New Mexico with a force of about 270 armed men and about fifty merchants. Historians argue about

Manuel Armijo, one of New Mexico's most controversial figures, served three terms as governor under Mexican administration. During the Mexican War, as U.S. troops approached Santa Fe, Armijo hastily fortified Apache Canyon, east of the city. He later changed his mind however, before any fighting took place and fled south without firing a shot. From the Shishkin Collection, NMSRCA

San Miguel del Vado was the last stop for travelers on the Santa Fe Trail before reaching New Mexico's capital. In 1841 several members of the Texas-Santa Fe expedition were imprisoned there following capture by militia forces. MNM (#13944)

just what the Texas invasion of New Mexico in 1841 was trying to do—or whether it was even an invasion. If Texas was trying to establish trade, why the troops? Or if it was an invasion, why the merchants? A leading theory is that they wanted to take over Santa Fe and thereby capture the lucrative Santa Fe Trail trade. (One historian finally gave up the argument and simply declared it a "harebrained scheme.")

The much-rumored, much-feared force approached New Mexico in the autumn of 1841. Governor Armijo—harassed by Indian attacks, governing a population that had revolted four years before, aware that Texas had special ties to the United States and therefore possibly to wealthy and influential traders in New Mexico, was ordered by Santa Anna to stop the invaders. He took his hastily assembled army out to meet them. The Texans turned out to be a pitiful lot. The poorly organized march from Texas had been a disaster. Lost, starved, and weak, the Texans were straggling up the Pecos River toward San Mi-

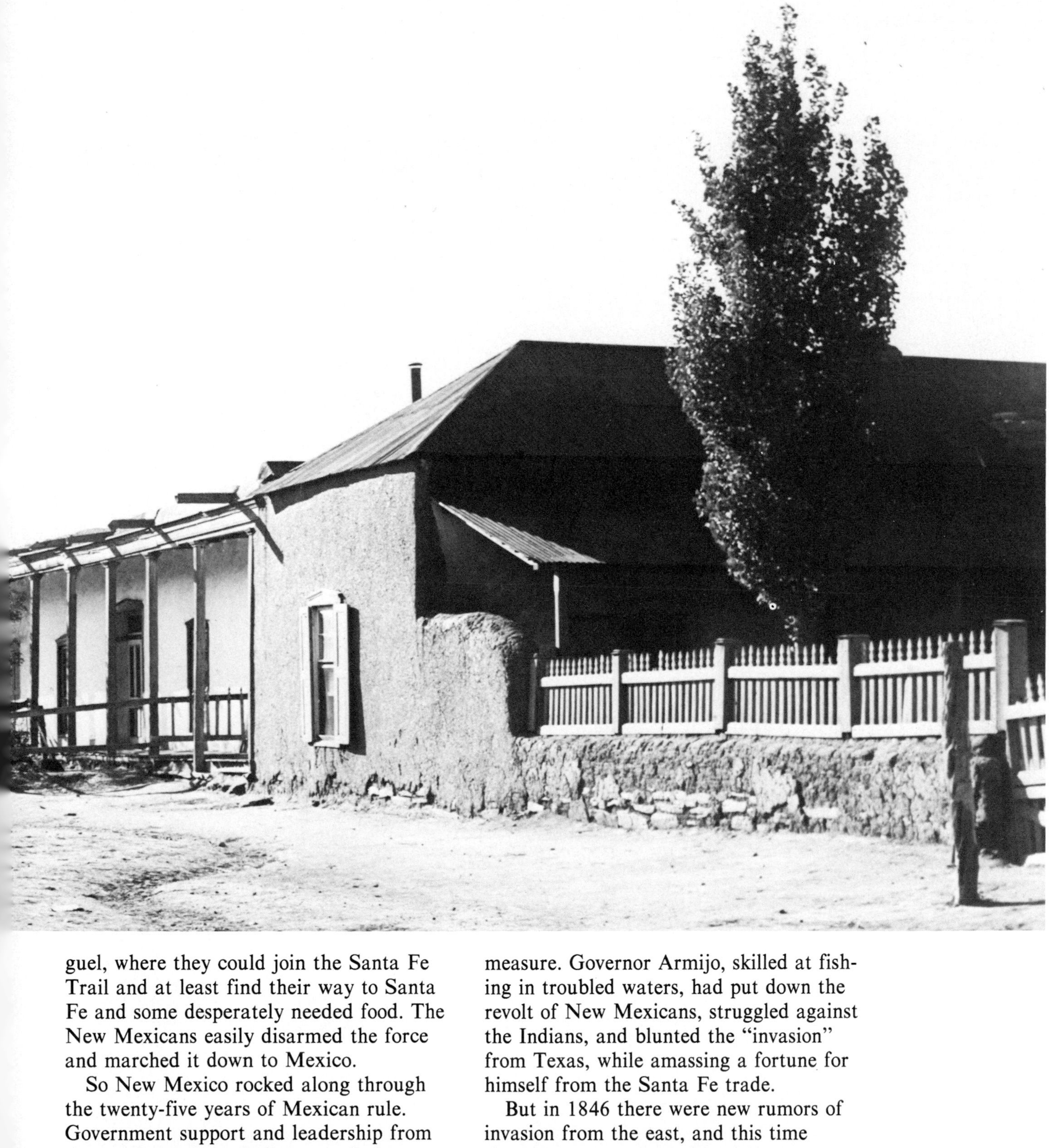

guel, where they could join the Santa Fe Trail and at least find their way to Santa Fe and some desperately needed food. The New Mexicans easily disarmed the force and marched it down to Mexico.

So New Mexico rocked along through the twenty-five years of Mexican rule. Government support and leadership from the south dried up. Indian attacks increased, and New Mexico was too weak and poor to do much about them. Wagons from the east kept coming through Glorieta Pass, bearing goods and ideas in like measure. Governor Armijo, skilled at fishing in troubled waters, had put down the revolt of New Mexicans, struggled against the Indians, and blunted the "invasion" from Texas, while amassing a fortune for himself from the Santa Fe trade.

But in 1846 there were new rumors of invasion from the east, and this time they were no exaggeration. An army was coming down the Santa Fe Trail, and a turning point was coming that would permanently change the future of New Mexico, Mexico, and the United States.

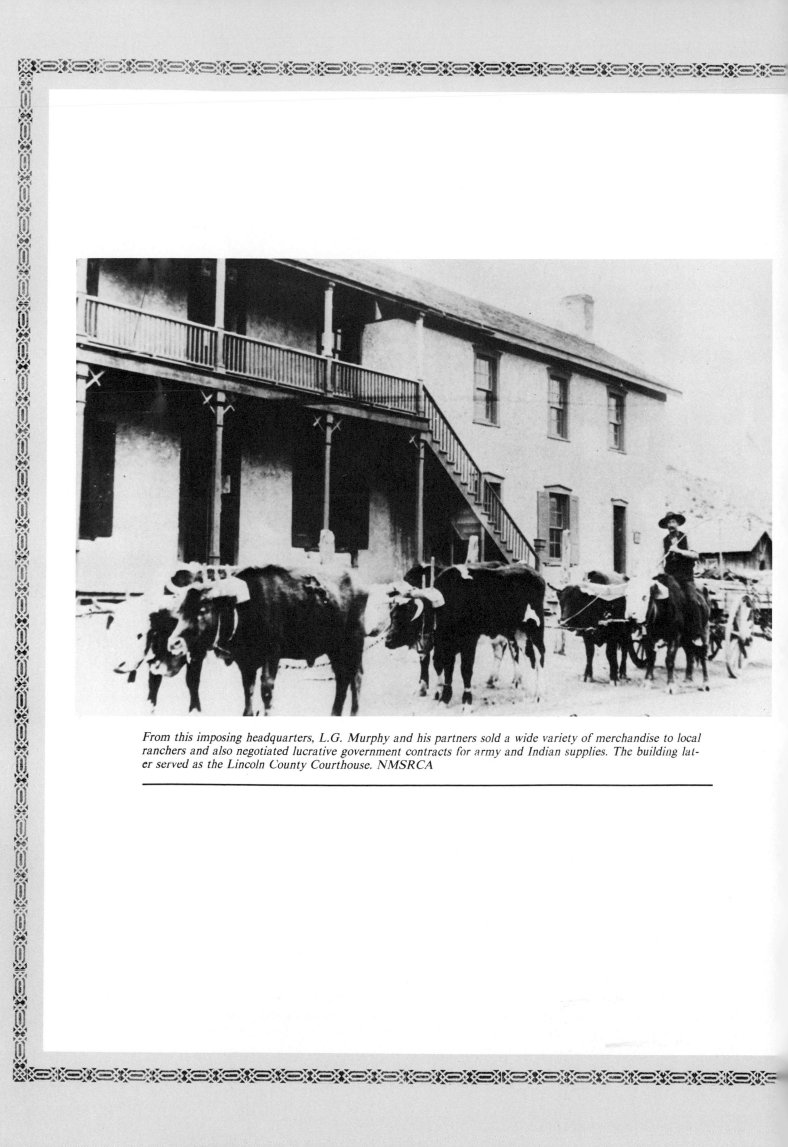

From this imposing headquarters, L.G. Murphy and his partners sold a wide variety of merchandise to local ranchers and also negotiated lucrative government contracts for army and Indian supplies. The building later served as the Lincoln County Courthouse. NMSRCA

New Mexico and the United States

President Polk had been elected with a mandate for U.S. territorial expansion, and he meant to fulfill it. A skirmish with Mexican troops in Texas was the spark, and on May 13, 1846, the United States declared war on Mexico. The next month tough, experienced Stephen Watts Kearny led a hastily assembled and provisioned "Army of the West" out of Fort Leavenworth, Kansas, and down the same Santa Fe Trail that had seen two decades of traders. In fact, some traders went along with the expedition, confident that whatever the outcome, they might still turn a profit.

Governor Armijo, sitting in the Palace of the Governors in Santa Fe, knew the troops were coming and debated what to do. He made brave noises about defense and issued ringing calls to the citizenry, but he probably knew that the invading army was too strong. Did he really want to resist it? For many staunch Catholic New Mexicans, the invaders were uncivilized Protestants, to be resisted at all costs. But most people were now using U.S. products in one way or another, and many—including Armijo himself—were locked into financial deals with U.S. merchants. Two brothers, long famous in the Santa Fe trade, accompanied the army. James Magoffin was along as an emissary of the U.S. Secretary of State, while his brother James (with his bride Susan, who kept a fascinating diary on the trip) brought along yet another wagon train.

Kearny's army paused at Bent's Old Fort, on the Arkansas River in Colorado, and Kearny sent James Magoffin on to talk with Governor Armijo. We do not know what passed between them, but it seems pretty clear that, one way or another, Magoffin was persuasive. The army continued its approach, pausing in Las Vegas long enough for Colonel Kearny to climb on a roof and announce the conquest of the territory, balancing the threat of force with promises of a new and just government. Still not sure what Armijo would do, Kearny marched his army into Glorieta Pass. Armijo was waiting with cannon and men at the west end of the canyon—a bottleneck the invaders would need to pass through in order to reach Santa Fe. But to the surprise of his own men, some of whom were furious, shortly before Kearny arrived at Armijo's defensive position, Armijo told the local militia to go home, and he himself rode off toward Mexico with the Mexican regulars. It has been an American fashion to disdain Armijo—conquerors have rarely been generous with those who lose. Until unexpected documents surface somewhere, we can only speculate as to why Armijo gave up. Perhaps Armijo was simply interested in delaying the Americans until the wagon train which he and another trader (an Anglo) owned was far enough south to escape the army. Perhaps he saw that the approaching army was too large to hope to defeat. The U.S. army proceeded unopposed and on August 18 raised the Stars and Stripes over Santa Fe. Political form had caught up with commercial reality.

Kearny improvised a government, named Charles Bent governor and installed other officials, and then took part

CHAPTER VI

Right
As a youth of seventeen, fresh from the midwest, Lewis H. Garrard accompanied an avenging party of mountain men from Bent's Fort to Taos. Although they arrived too late to take part in the battle at the pueblo, Garrard later wrote an eyewitness account of the trials and executions of rebel leaders. From the Garrard Collection, NMSRCA

Far right
When the Army of the West reached Bent's Fort on the Arkansas River, General S.W. Kearny sent James Wiley Magoffin (pictured), a trader with many contacts in New Mexico, on to Santa Fe to confer with Governor Armijo. No one knows what took place at their meeting, but soon afterwards Armijo abandoned his defenses and retreated to Mexico. MNM (#10310)

Bottom, far right
On May 13, 1846, President James Polk proclaimed that a state of war existed between the United States and Mexico. In late June Brigadier General Stephen Watts Kearny (pictured) led an expeditionary force known as the Army of the West out of Fort Leavenworth, Missouri, for the conquest of New Mexico and California. From the Shishkin Collection, NMSRCA

of his army and went to California, chasing Manifest Destiny. Actually New Mexico was not as acquiescent as he had expected. Especially in Taos the citizens resented the takeover by the United States. There were rumblings, and finally the outburst came. On January 19, 1847, men still loyal to Mexico, joined by Taos Pueblo Indians, killed Governor Bent in his home. Troops marched north from Santa Fe to put down the rebellion. It was bloody, possibly the more so because Bent had been a prominent and popular man—with the Anglo-Americans. The ruin of the church where the Indians took refuge still stands in the pueblo. The rebellion was over, leaving the United States in unquestioned control of distant New Mexico.

The people of Taos, especially the poor, had long had a champion in Padre Antonio José Martínez. Padre Martínez had the only printing press in New Mexico at the time (General Kearny's pronouncements were printed on it), which the priest had used to print religious material and material that espoused the causes and

rights of the poor. He was accused of having helped forment the rebellion, but it is more likely that his zeal reflected—but did not cause—local feeling.

The United States' control of New Mexico was confirmed after the War with Mexico by the Treaty of Guadalupe Hidalgo, signed on February 2, 1848. Once an outpost of Spain, then of Mexico, New Mexico now became a distant outpost of the United States.

There was still some patching up to do. The Treaty of Guadalupe Hidalgo left some land on the southwestern edge of New Mexico in dispute, area that lay athwart the route of a proposed railroad to California. The United States bought the land, known as the Gadsden Purchase, in 1853 for ten million dollars, and the continental United States (save Alaska) was basically filled out to the form it has today.

Meanwhile gold had been discovered in California, and it seemed the whole nation was heading west. Most of the "Forty-Niners" took the northern route, over the

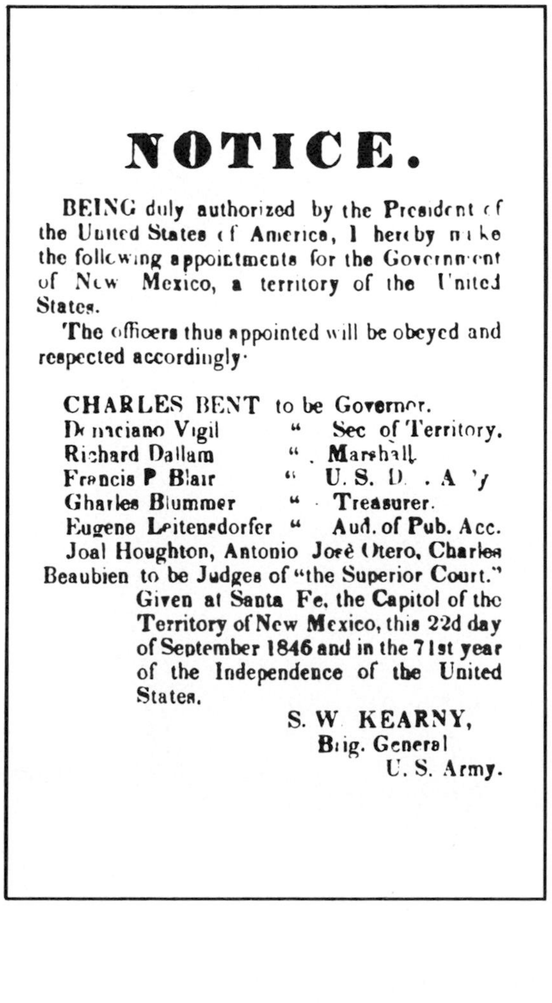

NOTICE.

BEING duly authorized by the President of the United States of America, I hereby make the following appointments for the Government of New Mexico, a territory of the United States.

The officers thus appointed will be obeyed and respected accordingly.

CHARLES BENT to be Governor.
Donaciano Vigil " Sec of Territory.
Richard Dallam " Marshall.
Francis P Blair " U. S. D. . A 'y
Gharles Blummer " Treasurer.
Eugene Leitensdorfer " Aud. of Pub. Acc.
Joal Houghton, Antonio José Otero, Charles Beaubien to be Judges of "the Superior Court."

Given at Santa Fe, the Capitol of the Territory of New Mexico, this 22d day of September 1846 and in the 71st year of the Independence of the United States.

S. W. KEARNY,
Brig. General
U. S. Army.

Above
On August 15, 1846, General Kearny and his staff rode into the plaza at Las Vegas where they were met by the local alcalde. *From the roof of this building Kearny announced that local officials would be retained in office after swearing allegiance to the U.S. From the Department of Development Collection, NMSRCA*

Left
On September 22, 1846, General Kearny issued a proclamation announcing his appointments for civil offices in New Mexico. From the Territorial Archives of New Mexico, NMSRCA

Oregon and California Trail, but many came through New Mexico. Regular stagecoach service from Missouri to Santa Fe began in 1849. With U.S. land law, lawyers came pouring in to establish offices and, they hoped, to grow with the territory. Increased protection from hostile Indians was one of the things General Kearny had promised, and in fact much effort and money was expended for that purpose. Indian raids weren't reduced by very much, but the numerous army posts, supply contracts, and surveying and road-building activities were an economic boon.

Along with the economic benefits of belonging to the United States came the political liability of being drawn into an implacable quarrel brewing to the east. Indian and Hispanic New Mexicans had no particular stake in the slavery issue; according to one record there were only twenty-two blacks in the entire territory, most of them servants of army officers. But Anglos (in New Mexico usage, "Anglo" refers to someone non-Hispanic and non-Indian, but not necessarily from the British Isles) were pouring in, bringing with them their affinities from home.

Above
Charles Bent, a former Santa Fe trader, was experienced in the region's business and political matters. This photograph of Charles Bent is a reproduction of a family miniature. From the Jaramillo-Bent Collection, NMSRCA

Right
While visiting his family during the winter of 1847, Governor Charles Bent was murdered by a band of Mexican nationalists and Indians from the pueblo of Taos. The Bent House is now a museum and art gallery. SHPB

Left
The rebellion of 1847 ended at the pueblo of Taos, where the insurgents barricaded themselves behind the thick adobe walls of the San Gerónimo mission. In the ensuing bombardment the church was almost completely destroyed, but the ruins are now preserved as a tribal monument. SHPB

Bottom
Despite Apache hostility, stage service expanded in the Southwest during the 1850s. As part of its long route from St. Louis to San Francisco, the Butterfield Overland Mail Company crossed Southern New Mexico. Today these ruins at Stein's Pass southwest of Lordsburg are all that remain of a once bustling station. SHPB

Above
In a region of great distances, livery stables provided an important service. This stable was built in 1883 and belonged to R.H. Cowan, a former stagecoach driver who settled at Springer. SHPB

Far Right
Henry H. Sibley, a West Point graduate from Louisiana, was commanding officer at Fort Union on the eve of the Civil War. Like many other Southern sympathizers, he resigned his commission and cast his lot with the Confederacy. MNM (#50541)

Many supported the Confederate cause.

General Henry Sibley, for instance, had been born in Louisiana and educated at West Point. In 1860 he was commandant at Fort Union, the important fort on the Santa Fe Trail a few miles north of Las Vegas, the traveler's first relief after the long prairie crossing. Now as the split neared, Sibley faced a hard choice. Would he stay with the Union, or go with the new Confederacy? Sibley chose the Confederacy, as did many other army officers of Southern birth, and approached Jefferson Davis, president of the Confederate States of America, with a proposal. He would raise an army of Texas volunteers and invade New Mexico, coming up the Rio Grande. The plan had some sense to it. There seemed little to stop Sibley from reaching the Colorado gold fields, which would relieve the Confederacy's strapped financial condition. From there he hoped to move west, capturing the California gold fields and establishing ports on the

Colonel Edward R.S. Canby (pictured) commanded Union forces in New Mexico. In the winter of 1862 Confederate troops under the command of Brigadier General H.H. Sibley marched up the Rio Grande from Texas and defeated Canby's men at the Battle of Valverde. From the McNitt Collection, NMSRCA

Pacific Coast to nullify the Union blockade of Southern ports. Plus, with a dramatic taking of half a continent early in the war, he hoped to sway France and England to side with the South. There is a flaw: modern strategists believe that even if Sibley had succeeded in the ambitious plan, he would have had too few men to govern the territory conquered. As it turned out, it never came to the test.

Sibley assembled his invasion force and came up the Rio Grande, entering New Mexico just above El Paso and occupying the Mesilla Valley and Fort Fillmore. At Valverde they met their first resistance from Colonel E.R.S. Canby, in charge of Union military forces defending New Mexico. The Confederates won, bypassing Fort Craig and the Union forces and heading toward Albuquerque. Colonel Canby found himself behind the Confederate army, pursuing them toward Albuquerque—which he was supposed to be defending. He sent word to have the Union supplies in Albuquerque destroyed before the Confederates could get them. His agents succeeded in destroying some, and some were destroyed by the Confederates themselves, who may have enjoyed too much the "spirits" available to them after a hard march. Leaving Albuquerque, Sibley split his forces and sent part through Tijeras Pass to head up the back side of the Sandia Mountains, while the other part went north and occupied Santa Fe. For the two weeks that the Confederates occupied the capital, New Mexico was, in effect, Confederate territory.

Meanwhile, telegrams had gone to Governor Gilpin of the Colorado territory, pleading with him to rush volunteers down to defend New Mexico. Because he was

Above
The chimneys of Fort Union still guard the plains north of Las Vegas. The fort was first built in 1851 and subsequently relocated twice. It was originally intended to protect the Santa Fe Trail and serve as a regional supply depot. NPS

Right
Troops stationed at Fort Union often retreated to Loma Parda for amusement. Although popular with the rank and file, the large number of dance halls, gambling dens and brothels enraged the fort's top brass. What is now left of Loma Parda is pictured in 1974. SHPB

Reinforced by Colorado volunteers, Union forces redeemed themselves in March of 1862 when they met the Confederates in a decisive battle near Glorieta Pass. Pigeon's Ranch, situated in Apache Canyon at the west end of the pass, was the site of sharp fighting and was occupied by both sides at various times. This photo of Pigeon's Ranch was taken circa 1900. From the Cultural Properties Review Committee Collection, NMSRCA

actually defending Colorado by doing so, Gilpin hastily complied. The Colorado Volunteers were a tough lot, many of them miners from the rapidly developing gold fields. They made an astonishing march, still one of the fastest in the annals of the U.S. Army. Leaving Denver on February 22, 1862, and marching down along the front range in snow and cold, they arrived at Fort Union on March 10. They had covered 400 miles—much of it through deep snow, and crossed Raton Pass—in thirteen days. At Fort Union they had a squabble with the man Canby had left in charge, about staying there to defend the fort, or moving on to seek the enemy. They chose the latter and, joined by forces from the fort, marched south along the Santa Fe Trail. By the night of March 25 they were at the east end of Glorieta Pass; they did not know it yet but Confederates were at the other end. There was a chance encounter of patrols in the pass and the next day a spirited skirmish. Now each army knew that a determined foe waited nearby. On the night of the twenty-seventh, men cleaned their guns and lay in the dark with eyes open; tomorrow would bring a battle.

The Union army moved into Glorieta Pass. About halfway through they stopped for rest and water at Pigeon's Ranch, a well-known way station on the Santa Fe Trail in more peaceful times. They had barely stacked their arms when the scouts sent ahead came running back. The enemy was just around the bend. Moments later the Confederate artillery came crashing in. Men grabbed their arms—or anyone's—and rushed into line.

The battle was bloody. Both sides had cannon, but much of the fighting was skirmishing in the brush. Overall the Confederates prevailed, forcing the Union back a mile or so.

But the seeming Confederate victory was to prove short-lived. At the beginning of the day one of the Colorado officers, Colonel John M. Chivington, had been detached with some 430 men to climb the heights alongside the canyon and circle behind the Confederate forces. Chivington,

In 1939 the Daughters of the Confederacy placed this monument near the village of Glorieta to commemorate the soldiers who fell in the battle fought there. The battle is sometimes called the "Gettysburg of the West." From the Department of Development Collection, NMSRCA

who had been a preacher in Colorado when he signed up for the volunteers, had refused a commission as chaplain, insisting that if he was going to be in the army, he would fight. With him were New Mexican volunteers led by Manuel A. Cháves, an experienced frontiersmen and fighter. For some reason Chivington went too far, and came out several miles behind the Confederate rear on the heights above the canyon mouth, looking down on the spot where sixteen years before Governor Armijo had stationed his men and then fled. Looking down now, Chivington's men saw the complete Confederate supply train, some 600 mules and 80 wagons, lightly guarded. There was most of the equipment of the invading army: ammunition, clothes, blankets, medicine, harnesses. It took but a few hours to complete the work of destruction. They burned the wagons and bayonetted the mules, and as darkness fell they went up onto the heights again and returned to the Union camp at the east end of the canyon.

The seeming Confederate victory had crumbled. An army could not live off the land in arid New Mexico, and there was nothing for the Confederates to do but straggle south. And straggle they did. Harassed by Canby, who had been joined by the victorious Fort Union forces, the Confederates buried two of their cannon in Albuquerque (they were dug up years later, and one is now in the Museum of Albuquerque), were defeated in a skirmish at Peralta, and eventually made their way back to Texas.

As army troops were pulled back east to fight in the Civil War, Apaches and Navajo, their freedom of movement and life ever more circumscribed by the culture burgeoning around them, reacted to the intolerable pressure by resuming raiding with a vengeance—which of course was intolerable to the surrounding culture. (The mirror image is not funny; it is tragic.) The army, in the person of General James H. Carleton, called in Kit Carson to solve the problem. Historians, novelists, and movie makers never have figured out just how to treat what happened then. It is impossible today to think with the mind of anyone who lived in those times, Indian or Anglo. We have the "facts"—probably more than they did—but we have experienced neither the horror of seeing our children killed and our property lost in a raid, nor the constant pressure of a culture for whom our right is their evil, our taboos their way of life. (The previous sentence can be read from either direction, the Indian and the Anglo-Hispanic looking at each other over a cultural abyss.) There were some on both sides who would have preferred annihilation as the final solution, and some even tried it. Carson, a remarkable man whose biographers are forced into extremes whether they are for him or against him, followed a middle ground. He

To implement his hardline Indian policy, General Carleton relied on New Mexico volunteers commanded by Colonel Christopher "Kit" Carson (pictured). After subduing the Mescalero Apaches in the summer of 1863, Carson began a vigorous campaign against the Navajos. From the Department of Development Collection, NMSRCA

pursued first the Apaches and then the Navajos, destroying their crops, cutting their fruit trees, and leaving them almost no alternative but to come into the tight, concentrated camp that the government prepared for them. (The Apaches left in a desperate move.) The camp was named for its lonely grove of trees along the trickling Pecos River in the sun-blasted east New Mexico plains: Bosque Redondo. The name and the "Long Walk" it took to get there live still in Navajo memory, not often spoken but not ever forgotten. Cramped, starving, humiliated, sick, the Navajo scratched the dry dirt in a futile effort at farming, and waited for the dole of food that was always short, either from bureaucratic bungling or outright fraud among the suppliers. Navajo children listened to yearning stories of the beautiful land of mesas and mountains they had come from. It was a tragedy, and perhaps the only conceivable alleviation in it is that the tribe did survive. In 1868 the government finally admitted that the experiment in forced farming was a failure. A treaty was signed and the Navajo began the trek home. There they rebuilt, accommodating that had to be made to the powerful culture which now shared their homeland. Today the Navajo are the largest Indian nation within the United States, their reservation mostly in Arizona but spilling into northwestern New Mexico. They seem to have the same problems making a bureaucracy work that the rest

Carleton hoped that the Navajos gathered at Bosque Redondo would learn to become farmers. His experiment failed, however, partly because the number of Indians confined there far exceeded preliminary estimates. From the McNitt Collection, NMSRCA

of the country has, and the desert is still a hard place to make a living. Still, tens of thousands of tourists annually see for themselves that it is indeed a beautiful land that they remembered and today inhabit again.

But in the complex web of the way humans get along—or don't—nothing can be isolated; everything affects everything else. At the army posts, Bosque Redondo, and other reservations there were people to be fed, and that meant a market for beef. Furthermore, the railroad was creeping across the plains from the east, and if you could get cattle to the railhead, your herds could be shipped back to eastern cities to be sold at a fine profit. Cattle raising boomed on the eastern plains. The opportunity was not lost on the ambitious, and not only New Mexicans. Note the players in the famous Lincoln County War: Colonel Emil Fritz, from Germany; James J. Dolan, Major Lawrence G. Murphy, and John G. Riley, all from Ireland; Alexander A. McSween, Canada; John G. Tunstall, England; and various other actors attracted by New Mexico's risky business opportunities. The Lincoln County War was the struggle for economic control of the county that developed into a series of shooting sprees. At least one element in the Lincoln County War was competition, pure and simple, for the contracts to supply beef and flour to various government markets. But also there was competition for political power and land, along with ethnic rivalries thrown in to add venom to ambition. The territorial government, dominated by the "Santa Fe Ring," was incapable of controlling the situation and, indeed, took sides and may have been responsible for some of the violence. The situation degenerated into gunfire and the Saturday-matinee drama of a burning house and a desperate breakout through "a hail of bullets." This time, however, it was not just a matinee, but real sons and husbands kicking and dying in the dirt. There is little noble in it, and it is strange that one of the characters, a possibly psychotic killer named William Bonney but nicknamed "Billy the Kid," has achieved mythological sainthood.

The Santa Fe Ring was unable or unwilling to control the Lincoln County War neutrally because it was not neutral. Historians differ in their interpretation of the ring—some even deny its existence—because no "ring" has a charter, outlining who is in it, who isn't, and what they are

for. Rather, in a troubled simmering pot there are enterprising people who see that, by cooperating, they may be able to grab a delectable morsel that is floating by. New Mexico had more than its share of enterprising people. Two names keep coming up in discussions of the Ring: "Smooth Steve" Stephen B. Elkins and "Tomcat" Thomas Catron. Both were lawyers, intelligent, ambitious, and active in politics. Politics means alliances, and they made them, with leading merchants, with county political leaders, and with corporations eager to do business in New Mexico. The alliances shifted with the project in hand; a foe in the election of a judge now might become an ally in a land deal later. And land deals were about the biggest opportunity going in New Mexico.

The problems of land ownership, which still plague New Mexico, were the direct result of one culture imposing its laws over another, which happened not once but twice, to thoroughly confuse the situation. The Indians had clear ideas, even with property markers, of what belonged to each pueblo. To a surprising degree, when the Spaniards came in they honored these, at least in reduced versions. To its own people Spain made individual and community "grants." These were not surveyed with anything approaching modern means, and trying to figure out where a "large cottonwood tree" used to be, or what "the skirt of the mountain" means, is problem enough. But even more troublesome was the Spanish idea of ownership. Individuals

Above
Supplies were seldom adequate at Fort Sumner to feed the Indians on the Bosque Redondo reservation. This circa 1866 Signal Corps photograph from the National Archives depicts a group of Navajos assembled for a head count. From the McNitt Collection, NMSRCA

Ellipse
Conflict between two rival factions for control of Lincoln County began shortly after the arrival of attorney Alexander A. McSween (pictured) in 1875. An aggressive and ambitious businessman, McSween soon found himself at odds with a small group of Civil War veterans headed by Lawrence G.

Ellipse
In 1876 Alexander A. McSween gained an important ally when a young Englishman named John H. Tunstall came to Lincoln. Tunstall, pictured in 1875, was searching for ranch investments and had just completed a tour of British Columbia and California. NMSRCA

Below
Once established in Lincoln, John G. Tunstall invested in grazing land and livestock. Encouraged by Alexander A. McSween, he erected a new building for his store, depicted in this photograph. NMSRCA

in a village owned their croplands, but by far the larger amount of the grant was used communally for pasture and wood gathering. Finally over this palimpsest came the United States, with its tidy ideas of clearly surveyed land, clearly conveyed to another person by a bill of sale, with much of it kept by the government as public lands. "Tidy," that is, if ownership was clear and agreed upon to begin with. It never was. How could the U.S. system cope with the concept of communal lands? Furthermore, too many of the persons involved had a personal stake in the outcome.

A case in point is the Maxwell Grant, which led into another "county war," the Colfax County War. Governor Manuel Armijo—who in the last days of the Mexican period had so many dealings with the Americans—had made the grant in the 1840s to a group headed by Charles Beaubien. Eventually ex-mountain man Lucien

Left ellipse
Soon after New Mexico achieved statehood, the legislature elected Thomas B. Catron to be one of its first U.S. senators. Catron, a Santa Fe attorney, is frequently identified as a leader of the Santa Fe Ring. From the Olsen Collection, NMSRCA

Far left ellipse
Stephen B. Elkins, a leader of the so-called Santa Fe Ring, was born in 1841 and graduated from the University of Missouri in 1860. In 1872 he became president of the Maxwell Land Grant and Railway Company and also served two terms as New Mexico's territorial delegate to Congress. Photo by Sarony, MNM (#10202)

Left
Lucien Maxwell's ranch was a popular stopping place on the mountain branch of the Santa Fe Trail in the 1860s. From this base Maxwell consolidated the claims of various heirs to the Beaubien-Miranda land grant, which he sold in 1870 to an investment syndicate for $1,350,000. The ranch is pictured in this circa 1940 painting. From the School of American Research Collection, NMSRCA

Now a ghost town south of Lordsburg, Shakespeare was once Ralston, a lively mining camp. In 1872 the area received a lot of bad publicity because of a diamond salting scheme intended to swindle unwary investors. To improve the town's image, its name was changed from Ralston to Shakespeare in 1879. The town is pictured as it appeared in 1973. SHPB

Maxwell, Beaubien's son-in-law, bought it, but it was not clear exactly what he had bought. Was it two million acres? Or one-twentieth of that? Both figures had their adherents. The grant was roughly Colfax County, up on the northeast border. The visitor driving in today on I-25, after coming over Raton Pass, drives through the Maxwell Grant for the next hour or so. Early on, the United States Secretary of the Interior had ruled that the grant would be limited to 97,000 acres due to an old Mexican law, and settlers promptly claimed the other part. (Many had already moved onto it, believing it to be public land.) Here is where the cooperative effort afforded by the Ring was crucial. A state surveyor—a Ring man—surveyed the grant out at the two-million-acre figure, instantly outraging the settlers then threatened with displacement. The resulting mess was in the courts for years. "Smooth Steve" Elkins became president of a company competing with rival groups to control the land, and ran for Congress (and won) largely to promote its interests. There were killings, and even the prosecutions which followed seem to have been politically controlled. The issue was too big to die quietly, and eventually another survey, by Elkins' brother, reduced the inflammatory two million acres to a "mere" 1.7 million. Eventually this figure held up,

although the bitterness can still occasionally be heard.

In the decades following the Civil War, the United States became aware of the West. By 1878 the Atchison, Topeka & Santa Fe Railroad and its rival, the Denver & Rio Grande Western, had both reached Pueblo, Colorado, and began a race to see who would first claim the best route south, along "Uncle Dick" Wootton's toll road over Raton Pass into New Mexico. AT&SF men had lobbied the legislature in Santa Fe all the previous session to get a charter for their New Mexico subsidiary. During the autumn an AT&SF civil engineer named William R. Morley, pretending to be a sheepherder so as not to rouse the suspicions of D&RG men, had pretty well figured out the route and grades over the pass. According to one of those dramatic stories of the West that just may be true, both lines sent crews to the little town of El Moro at the foot of the Colorado side of the pass on a cold night in February 1878. While the D&RG crew lodged for the night in the hotel, the AT&SF men went on up the hill to "Uncle Dick" Wootton's and made a deal. They moved a few shovelfuls of dirt and by dawn claimed the pass by right of first construction. The total compensation paid to Wootton was a lifetime pass on the railroad and twenty-five dollars a month for groceries—later increased to seventy-five dollars.

The first locomotive entered the terri-

Formerly a stage station known as Willow Springs, Raton began to grow soon after the Atchison, Topeka, and Santa Fe tracks crossed Raton Pass in 1878. This photograph shows First Street in the 1880s, with railway company buildings in the foreground. From the Raton Museum Photo Collections

In 1877 William R. Morley established the present route of the Santa Fe Railroad. According to tradition he prevented rivals with the Denver & Rio Grande Railroad from learning his plan by disguising himself as a sheepherder while completing his survey. MNM (#77764)

tory about December 1, 1878. For a while the engine that pulled loads over the pass was the most powerful in the world, appropriately enough called the "Uncle Dick." The line pushed south past Las Vegas and then turned west into Glorieta Pass following the route of the old Santa Fe Trail, still the most logical way through the mountains. But by now a simple fact of geography and engineering had become obvious: you could not get to Santa Fe without going up a hill. As a result, the Santa Fe Railroad decided to bypass Santa Fe and go directly to Albuquerque where, with the legal and financial cooperation of city fathers, the railroad had decided to build its regional depot and yards. It was obvious now that the railroad's main goal was the Pacific coast, and New Mexico was just a way station. Afraid it might be left to wither on—off—the vine, Santa Fe civic leaders, including the famous Bishop Lamy whose signature was first on the petition circulated to voters, floated a bond issue and succeeded in procuring a branch line. Bishop Lamy also owned the land where the connection was made, and the little town there today is called Lamy.

The line pushed on down the Rio Grande and approached Albuquerque. The railroad had decided to build its regional depot and yards in Albuquerque. Here is one of the fascinating "what-might-have-beens" of history. AT&SF officials had first wanted to build terminal facilities in Bernalillo, but venerable José Leandro Perea, *patron* of that settlement, had demanded too high a price for the land they needed. Why did he do this? For one, a wealthy man, Perea did not need the money. Also, it is entirely possible that the progress promised by the railroad did not strike him as progress at all, and he would as soon have had it built somewhere else. If that was his wish, he succeeded. Triggered by the coming of the railroad, Albuquerque began rushing to become the major city it is today; and Bernalillo continued to be . . . what it is now. An argument as to who won would have passionate supporters on each side.

There was more railroad building to be done, although an astonishing one-third of New Mexico's trackage was built from 1879 to 1881. The Denver & Rio Grande Western did eventually get lines into the state, one coming down from the San Luis Valley and reaching Santa Fe from the north, the other crossing the northern part of the state to its terminus in Durango. (After the freight business fell off, a part of this narrow-gauge northern line was converted to a tourist attraction, now one of the finest ways to see that part of the

Left
Accompanied by other French-born ecclesiastics, Archbishop Jean Baptiste Lamy (standing, with cane in hand) enjoys his garden on a summer afternoon. Joseph Priest Machbeuf, his protégé and confidant, is standing to the far right. Jean Baptiste Salpointe, who succeeded Lamy as archbishop, is seated to the left. From the Farrar Collection, NMSRCA

Bottom, left
After emerging from the narrow confines of Apache Canyon, the main line of the Santa Fe Railroad continued southwest through Galisteo Basin toward Albuquerque, instead of climbing the steep grade up to the city of Santa Fe. Despite outraged protests from civic leaders, New Mexico's capital had to content itself with a branch line. Photo by George C. Bennett, MNM (#37441)

Bottom, right
In 1880 the Denver & Rio Grande Railroad constructed one of the most difficult routes into New Mexico, a branch that extended over Cumbres Pass from Antonito, Colorado, to Chama. From Chama, the narrow gauge line continued on to the Colorado mining towns of Durango and Silverton. SHPB

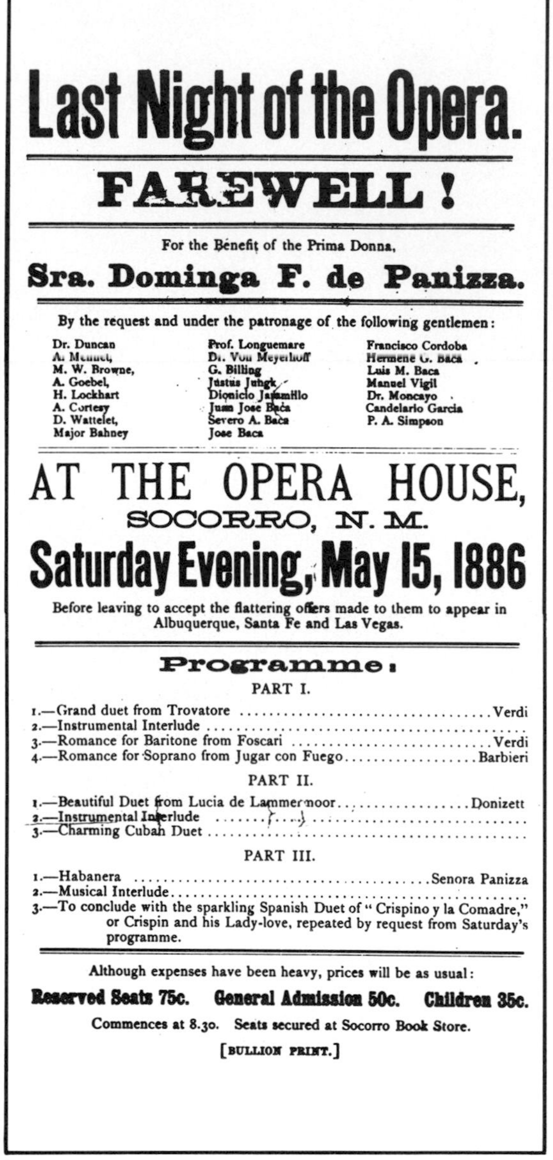

Last Night of the Opera.

FAREWELL !

For the Benefit of the Prima Donna,

Sra. Dominga F. de Panizza.

By the request and under the patronage of the following gentlemen:

Dr. Duncan	Prof. Longuemare	Francisco Cordoba
A. Mennet,	Dr. Von Meyerhoff	Hermene G. Baca
M. W. Browne,	G. Billing	Luis M. Baca
A. Goebel,	Justus Jungk	Manuel Vigil
H. Lockhart	Dionicio Jaramillo	Dr. Moncayo
A. Cortesy	Juan Jose Baca	Candelario Garcia
D. Wattelet,	Severo A. Baca	P. A. Simpson
Major Bahney	Jose Baca	

AT THE OPERA HOUSE,
SOCORRO, N. M.

Saturday Evening, May 15, 1886

Before leaving to accept the flattering offers made to them to appear in Albuquerque, Santa Fe and Las Vegas.

Programme:

PART I.

1.—Grand duet from Trovatore .... Verdi
2.—Instrumental Interlude ....
3.—Romance for Baritone from Foscari .... Verdi
4.—Romance for Soprano from Jugar con Fuego .... Barbieri

PART II.

1.—Beautiful Duet from Lucia de Lammermoor .... Donizett
2.—Instrumental Interlude ....
3.—Charming Cuban Duet ....

PART III.

1.—Habanera .... Senora Panizza
2.—Musical Interlude ....
3.—To conclude with the sparkling Spanish Duet of "Crispino y la Comadre," or Crispin and his Lady-love, repeated by request from Saturday's programme.

Although expenses have been heavy, prices will be as usual:

Reserved Seats 75c. General Admission 50c. Children 35c.

Commences at 8.30. Seats secured at Socorro Book Store.

[BULLION PRINT.]

Right
Like Americans everywhere, New Mexico's citizens hungered for culture in the late nineteenth century. Even grand opera found its way to the frontier. Traveling companies such as this one at Socorro brightened the theatrical season with selections from Verdi and Bizet. Courtesy, Socorro Historical Society

Far right
A pioneer archeologist and ethnohistorian, Adolph F. Bandelier was born in Berne, Switzerland, in 1840. He first visited New Mexico in 1880. Subsequently he conducted the first comprehensive survey of the region's prehistoric ruins. During his investigations he traveled thousands of miles on foot or horseback, remaining at various Indian villages for weeks at a time. From the Ramona Indian School Collection. Courtesy, University of New Mexico General Library, Special Collections

state.) Tracks were laid on down the river to El Paso by the AT&SF, and in two main corridors it went west and connected to California. As agriculture and later minerals were developed in the southeastern plains, steel rails were laid there too.

What did the railroad do for New Mexico? It is almost incalculable. Before, New Mexico had been a distant place. All of the ways to get here had been hard: the six- to nine-month ox-cart trek from Mexico City in the seventeenth century, the long plodding of the freight caravans across the plains from Kansas City, and—not much better—the gut-wrenching sway-ride of the stagecoach. Suddenly, getting to New Mexico was a matter of two or three days. Freight rates dropped dramatically. Goods from the East poured in, and prices dropped. (Historian Marc Simmons has documented what the new rates did just for the sheep industry, with easy transportation of wool.) People, too, could come more easily, their way made almost luxurious by the railroad's genius of profitable hospitality, Fred Harvey. The diary of an anthropologist (another species the railroad began bringing in quantity) is telling. Adolf Bandelier stepped down from the train in Lamy in August 1880, the first year of the train's existence. Two years later he came again and on March 19, 1882, wrote in his diary after walking around Santa Fe, "the city has

Despite its luxurious accommodations the Montezuma Hotel was not a financial success. After its sale by the Santa Fe, the Montezuma changed hands several times and was occupied by a wide variety of tenants. Recently remodeled, it now houses a branch of United World College. From the Department of Development Collection, NMSRCA

grown considerably. New houses have sprung up, some two-story . . . with metallic roofs." (Those tin roofs were one more product brought by the railroad, for it was expensive to haul sheets of tin from Kansas City via freight wagon.) It is not true to say that the railroad was the end of the Santa Fe Trail. Freight, people, and ideas still made their way in both directions across the prairies, tying this distant place to the more populous East. Santa Fe was married to the rest of the United States, as the ceremony says, for better or worse.

With the railroads and modern extraction methods, mining finally came into its own. From the beginning, European explorers had pursued the shining vision of gold and silver, but for the most part New Mexico's ore deposits proved disappointing. One notable exception was (and is) the great Santa Rita copper mine in the southwest corner of the state. In 1800 an Apache Indian guide showed Spanish Lieutenant Colonel José Manuel Carrasco the copper deposits, and the next year Spaniards began working the mine, sending the ore to Chihuahua and Mexico City by burro trains. Apache troubles closed the workings at various times. Eventually the "easy" copper gave out, but when open-pit methods were developed around 1910, the Santa Rita mine became one of the largest open-pit operations in the world.

Right
Determined prospectors panned for gold along New Mexico's streams and canyons in the last decades of the nineteenth century. Water was an indispensable element in placer mining. From the McDonald Collection, NMSRCA

Below
Despite frequent military campaigns conducted against the Apache by Spanish, Mexican, and United States troops, warriors fought for their rights in the Southwest for three centuries. From the McNitt Collection, NMSRCA

Other dramatic but generally short-lived strikes have punctuated New Mexico's history. Not far from Santa Rita is Silver City, a town much like many other New Mexico towns today, but a legendary place in its heyday. Prospectors finding themselves suddenly rich imported an orchestra from San Francisco to play in a rough, roaring mining town still experiencing Apache raids, and at the mere rumor of a new strike the town would empty of able-bodied men in a few hours. Yet that is not the whole story of this mining town. Wealth dug from the ground built a solid community of more than brick houses. Silver City developed a library and an outstanding early educational system. It was a "boomtown," but its citizens made it last.

In 1828 gold was discovered in the Ortiz Mountains south of Santa Fe, and a minor rush followed. The Ortiz gold fields, too, soon gave out, largely because of the difficulty of obtaining water for the necessary processing. Thomas Edison erected a processing plant there in the late 1800s, trying to use static electricity to extract the gold, but the attempt failed. Technolo-

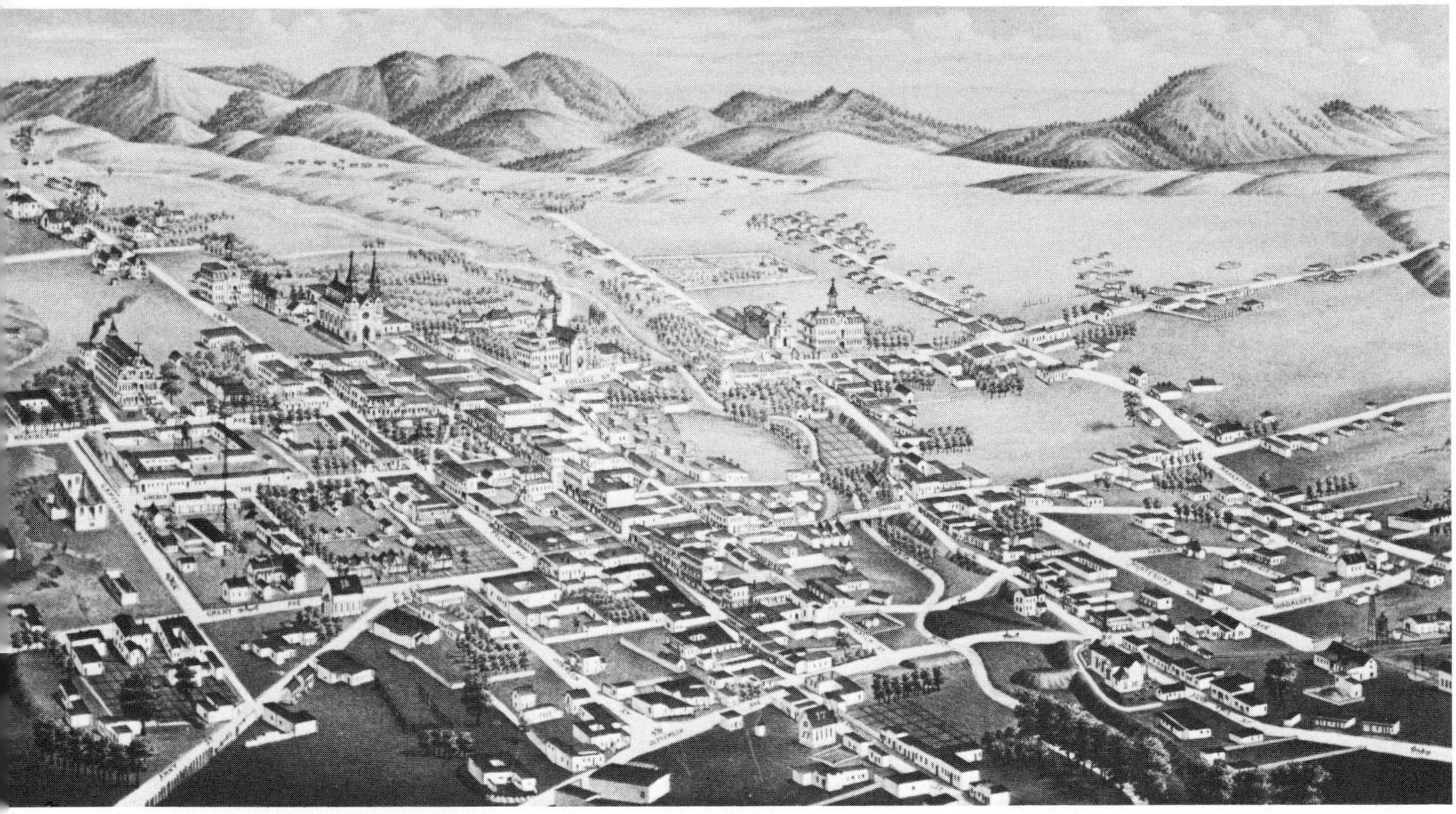

Above
American artist Henry Wellge (1850-1917) drew Bird's Eye View of the City of Santa Fe, N.M. *in 1882. Courtesy, Amon Carter Museum, Fort Worth*

Left
Maintenance of law and order sometimes required strong measures by local officials to restrain nineteenth-century desperadoes. This jail, located in Tomé, a village south of Albuquerque, has walls four feet thick made of volcanic rock covered with adobe. Erected in 1875, Tomé Jail is all that remains of a larger building that served for a short time as the Valencia County Courthouse. SHPB

Centuries after the Anasazi abandoned it, Navajos occupied Chaco Canyon. These horsemen rode into pueblo Bonito in 1891 for a celebration staged by Richard Wetherill, who operated a trading post there. Wetherill—a famous amateur archeologist—and his brothers discovered the awesome ruins at Mesa Verde, Colorado, in 1888. From the McNitt Collection, NMSRCA

gy has at last caught up, however, and today a modern mining operation uses complex, electrolytic technology to recover gold too fine to be seen by the naked eye.

Gold was discovered at Elizabethtown in the Maxwell Land Grant, but again there was no water to process the ore, despite heroic attempts at building "the Big Ditch," which wound forty-one miles to bring water from eleven miles away. White Oaks in Lincoln County had its heyday, but today it is windblown and almost abandoned. One of the great legends—this one true—is of the "Bridal Chamber." This incredible chamber, discovered in a mine near Hillsboro in the 1880s, yielded more than three million dollars—in 1880 dollars—of horn (free, almost pure) silver. A spur line was run into the chamber and silver was simply loaded directly onto the cars. The area just west of Socorro proved rich in lead, zinc, copper, and silver, and attracted another "run," which proved more permanent. In 1889 the legislature created the School of Mines in Socorro, now the New Mexico Institute of Mining and Technology.

To realize the true value of minerals in New Mexico, however, one must escape the hypnotic effect of the romantic two, gold and silver. Carlsbad has long had an industry in potash; it may be less dramatic, but fortunes have been built upon it. When the nation discovered the secret power of uranium, rich deposits around Grants created a boom that lasted for two decades but which, like so many other mining booms, has declined drastically. New Mexico's greatest long-term mining potential probably lies in her reserves of fossil fuels: coal in the northwest corner of the state, and oil and natural gas both there and in the southeast.

New Mexico's growth, from a distant colony of Mexico to a valued U.S. territory with vast economic opportunities and natural resources, would only continue in the coming years of statehood.

Above
School construction increased rapidly after 1891. Youthful scholars struggled with "the three Rs" in buildings like this one at White Oaks, a gold-mining town northeast of Carrizozo. SHPB

Left
During the 1880s and 1890s many new industries began operations in New Mexico, including Albuquerque's Southwestern Brewery and Ice Company. After its completion in 1899, this handsome, five-story building was the tallest in the territory, according to the local press. SHPB

President William Howard Taft stopped briefly in Albuquerque while enroute to a conference with Mexican President Porfirio Díaz in 1909. On October 15 a large crowd of citizens gathered at the Alvarado Hotel to greet the President. A banquet that evening was marked by a sharp exchange concerning statehood for New Mexico between Taft and politician Albert B. Fall. From the Hubbell Collection, NMSRCA

One of the Fifty

New Mexico was now bound to the United States, for better or worse, by railroad ties and tracks of steel. To risk stretching a metaphor too far, would the union be legitimated with the gold of statehood? Since 1850, or 1846 if you count General Kearny's makeshift government, New Mexico had been a territory, and it was to remain in that status longer than any other part of the nation. In six decades, supporters of statehood managed to get more than fifty statehood bills introduced in Congress; none of them succeeded. There is a story that one bill was defeated because the territorial representative, "Smooth Steve" Elkins, mistakenly shook hands with a Northern reconstructionist congressman, thereby alienating Southern representatives. Of course there is more to it than that. Some local merchants worried that taxes would increase once federal support given to territories ceased. Local officials feared they would lose their political power. Still, by and large the citizens did want statehood, and New Mexico repeatedly called constitutional conventions and drafted constitutions to present to the federal government. Nothing happened.

The federal government found itself with a knotty problem, some aspects of which were not easily discussed. The general pattern of U.S. expansion had been to acquire "blank" (Indian-occupied) territory, settle it, and absorb it as a new state—rather like welcoming back into the firm a son who had gone out and started his own company. Now, for the first time, the United States was being asked to absorb a preexisting, alien culture that was in fact much older than the United States itself. The problem of land law and communal ownership was only one manifestation of the dilemma. There were also the questions of language and religion, as an essentially Protestant, English-speaking nation looked with suspicion upon a Spanish-speaking, Roman Catholic enclave where in 1890 almost all of the schools were parochial and the church supplied the teachers for the rest. Suspicions were compounded by stories of shootings and hangings and of those "county wars," although other territories—Missouri, for example, which became wealthy on the Santa Fe trade—had been made a state while it was still notoriously lawless.

These problems stymied all attempts at statehood for more than half a century. Still, one by one they were met, battered down, or smoothed over. Finally, on January 6, 1912, New Mexico became the forty-seventh state in the union. William C. McDonald of White Oaks was elected the first state governor of New Mexico.

New Mexico now found itself fully joined to the United States, while heritage and geography still tied it to Mexico. It is not surprising that Mexican troubles spilled across the border. In 1916, during a period of revolution in Mexico, the U.S. government supported one side, thoroughly alienating the famous Pancho Villa, who was attempting to take control. Either from spite over his rejection by the U.S. State Department, or perhaps in a subtle plot to force the United States to invade Mexico and thus oppose his rival Venustiano Carranza, early on the morning of March 9, 1916, Pancho Villa's forces raided the New Mexican border town of Columbus. He got his invasion. Brigadier General John J. "Black Jack" Pershing entered Mexico with 7,000 men to pursue Villa. He never caught up with Villa but

CHAPTER VII

Right
Maintenance and repair of railroad equipment brought heavy industry to New Mexico for the first time. Albuquerque's Atlantic & Pacific shops gave the town a substantial payroll. Eventually the Atlantic & Pacific became part of the Santa Fe system. From the Department of Development Collection, NMSRCA

Below
With the expansion of railroad lines in the 1880s, New Mexico's range cattle industry boomed. This 1914 painting by Taos artist Oscar E. Berninghaus portrays a group of cowboys relaxing at the chuckwagon during a roundup. NMSRCA

Left
When the Spanish-American War broke out in 1898, New Mexico quickly filled its enlistment quota, following President William McKinley's call for volunteers. Commanded by Lieutenant-Colonel Theodore Roosevelt, these troops became known as roughriders. The contingent pictured traveled to San Antonio, Texas, for training. It is easy to see from this photo that patriotic fever ran high. From the Adelia Collier Collection, NMSRCA

Bottom
Although modest in size, Santa Rosa's first bank was an object of civic pride. When rumors spread that deperadoes intended a holdup, local citizens stood guard around the institution and foiled the scheme. From the Cultural Properties Review Committee Collection, NMSRCA

Above
Ratified by the voters on January 21, 1911, New Mexico's first constitution was extremely conservative. Unlike similar documents approved by other Western states, it had no provisions for such democratic reform measures as initiative, recall, or women's suffrage. Photo by William R. Walton, MNM (#8119)

Opposite, top
In 1907 a group of politicians enroute to the inauguration of Governor Curry posed for a photograph. The tall man in the back row is Pat Garrett, who shot and killed Billy the Kid. To Garrett's right is William C. McDonald. Third from the right in the front row sits Albert B. Fall. NMSRCA

Opposite, bottom
Hoping to limit damage, local citizens organized fire companies such as this one, pictured in 1905. From the Cobb Collection. Courtesy, University of New Mexico General Library, Special Collections

Right
Appointed governor of New Mexico by President William McKinley in 1897, Miguel A. Otero was the only Hispano to hold that position prior to statehood. Otero served until 1906, the longest term of any chief executive. When the Spanish-American War broke out in 1898, Otero's enthusiastic response to the call for volunteers caused New Mexico's quota of roughriders to be raised within a few days. From the Otero Collection. Courtesy, University of New Mexico General Library, Special Collections

Santa Fe

Right
William C. McDonald, New Mexico's first governor after statehood, came to New Mexico from upstate New York in 1880. McDonald, a surveyor and rancher, resided at White Oaks in Lincoln County when elected to the state's highest executive office. MNM (#50589)

Top, far right
Before dawn on March 9, 1916, followers of Mexican caudillo *Francisco "Pancho" Villa struck the border town of Columbus. Despite initial success, the raiders encountered strong resistance from the U.S. Army garrison and were forced to withdraw. Eighteen Americans and approximately one hundred Mexicans were killed in the attack. NMSRCA*

Bottom
On January 15, 1912, William C. McDonald was inaugurated as governor before a throng of enthusiastic citizens. Chief Justice Clarence J. Roberts administered the oath of office. MNM (#27293)

did run into Mexican national forces at Parral. Seven U.S. soldiers were killed, and hotheads on both sides called for war. Cooler heads prevailed, partly because war was coming—in Europe. Pershing's forces withdrew from Mexico, and further bloodshed was avoided.

The war in Europe, which overshadowed the fuss with Pancho Villa, reached New Mexico too. A State Council of Defense was created to help with the effort, although the $75,000 they made available seems remarkably small by today's standards. Approximately 17,000 New Mexicans served in the armed forces, perhaps the strongest proof possible, if any were needed, that New Mexico was a full-fledged part of the United States.

The Great Depression of the 1930s hit New Mexico hard, especially in coal production: in four years the tonnage mined dropped by 72 percent. Later, as trains

Far left
Octoviano A. Larrazolo was elected governor in 1918. At the end of his term, he created a storm of controversy when he pardoned sixteen Villistas. From the State Officials Collection. Courtesy, University of New Mexico General Library, Special Collections

Below
Following Pancho Villa's raid on Columbus, President Woodrow Wilson ordered General John Pershing to lead an expeditionary force in pursuit of the famous bandit. MNM (#5816)

Above
Although Pancho Villa managed to elude Pershing's troops, the "Punitive Expedition" gave the army an opportunity to test new equipment. From the Farrar Collection, NMSRCA

Far right
Albert B. Fall, a veteran legislator and judge, held office under both political parties. Fall's career ended in disgrace, due to his role as President Warren G. Harding's Secretary of Interior in the Teapot Dome oil scandal. From the Olsen Collection, NMSRCA

converted to diesel, coal town after coal town shut down. Nevertheless, coal lies beneath some one-fifth of New Mexico's surface, and such an energy source could not be ignored for very long. Modern technologies for strip mining, as well as demands for the low-sulphur coal available in the state, brought about a resurgence of the San Juan Basin in the 1970s. The coal reserves there lie near the surface, easily strippable; on satellite photographs one can actually see a relatively dark band arcing from Farmington southeastward, formed by the numerous outcroppings of coal on the surface. Now the coal is used not for running trains or heating homes, but for the production of electricity. New Mexico itself consumes only about one-third the electrical power it produces, the rest leaving (as have many of New Mexico's sons and daughters) for the lights of big cities elsewhere.

The petroleum industry is a relatively

Left
From the arrival of the railroads until the end of World War II, coal mining was an important industry in New Mexico. While coal enjoyed a strong demand for industrial and home heating purposes, company towns such as Madrid grew up beside the mines in which the corporation controlled every aspect of life. From the McKittrick Collection, NMSRCA

Bottom, left
Since the 1920s petroleum production has been important in Southeastern New Mexico's economy. The region, known as Little Texas, *is heavily dependent on the oil and gas industry. This Continental-Shell refinery near Hobbs extracted highly volatile "casinghead" gasoline from natural gas, which was then blended with lower grades to produce a fuel suitable for automobiles. From the Department of Development Collection, NMSRCA*

Bottom, right
During the 1920s the oil and gas business began to boom in New Mexico, particularly in the state's southeast and northwest quadrants. The exploration shown here took place near Shiprock in San Juan County. From the Department of Development Collection, NMSRCA

The huge open-pit copper mine at Santa Rita is one of Southwestern New Mexico's most important industries. Although the mine was worked by Chihuahua entrepreneurs in the early 1800s, it was not until after 1910 that mechanization permitted extensive exploitation of the rich mineral deposits. The unusual geological formation on the horizon is called "The Kneeling Nun." From the Department of Development Collection, NMSRCA

young one, its growth reflecting that of the internal combustion engine. In 1928 New Mexico produced 1.2 million barrels of oil; in 1983 the figure was more than seventy-one million barrels. The state has two main petroleum and natural gas producing areas: the San Juan Basin in the northwest, and the southeastern region centered around Carlsbad, an area known to geologists as the Permian Basin. Both of these corners of the state have experienced the "boom and bust" cycles of the industry, but the trend has been steadily upward, and today New Mexico is one of the leading energy producing states in the union.

New Mexico's natural resources have been an economic boon, not only in providing minerals and fuels but also in attracting people. Early train passengers may have reached the state more quickly than they would have in stagecoaches, but conditions were not that much better. Meal stops were hurried, the food generally awful. Then a genius named Fred Harvey took over passenger services for the line, and soon Harvey Houses (and their carefully chosen, hardworking attendants, "Harvey Girls") were famous among grateful travelers.

The favorable publicity attracted visitors, many of whom wanted to see more of the fascinating country glimpsed through a train window. Thus there developed a business in short automobile tours to Indian pueblos and other attractions, known as the Indian Detours, with well-trained guides and well-equipped cars. Throughout the 1920s thousands of visitors from the East had the pleasure of an Indian Detour. The Indian Detour finally disappeared, a victim of the Depression and the rise of the private automobile, but by then the nation as a whole was aware of the Southwest. Calendars in every state carried pic-

Completed in 1898, the Castañeda was one of a series of luxury hotels built by the Santa Fe Railroad and operated by the Fred Harvey Company. An English immigrant, Harvey developed a profitable business by providing tourists with pleasing meals and accomodations. To staff his dining rooms Harvey hired attractive, courteous waitresses known as "Harvey girls." He also established Indian Detours, a guide service for travelers desiring side trips to points of interest in New Mexico and Arizona. Photo by Edward Kemp. MNM (#46947)

Cattle ranching has been an important element to New Mexico's economy for more than one hundred years. For all working cowboys branding livestock is part of the regular ranch routine. The Tom Mix hats these San Gabriel Ranch cowpokes are wearing date this photo to around the 1920s. Photo by Edward Kemp, MNM (#53705)

Above
The Christmas lighting display that brightens Albuquerque's Old Town Plaza is one of the city's most popular attractions for both residents and visitors alike. ACVB

Right
Since Spanish colonial times Navajo blankets have always been among the most sought after of Southwestern Indian crafts. Today they bring higher prices than ever before because of recent interest in indigenous artifacts. From the Bullock Collection, NMSRCA

tures of a Santa Fe train dwarfed by mesas and desert, or of Indians in colorful dress against breathtaking scenery. New Mexico had created an image in the national consciousness as a place of wonderful light, of colorful, mysterious people, and of a romantic almost-lost way of life.

Artists were attracted to the image—and the reality—of New Mexico. A broken wagon wheel stopped two artists on their way to Mexico in 1898, and they "discovered" Taos. Bert Phillips and Ernest Blumenschein wrote their friends about the wonderful light, the incredible vistas, and the fascinating Indian ceremonials. Some came to see for themselves and stayed, living in adobe houses on dirt lanes. Taos found itself with an artists' colony, of residents who painted when the light was high—and partied when it was not. The intellectual ferment attracted writers as well. Perhaps the most famous was D.H. Lawrence, who came to Taos as the guest of that remarkable heiress, Mabel Dodge Luhan, and, like so many

Above
After an apprenticeship at New York's Art Students League, W. Herbert "Buck" Dunton came to Taos in 1912. His paintings interpreted the American West. From the School of American Research Collection, NMSRCA

Left
Refurbishing a house's walls with a new coat of adobe plaster has traditionally been regarded as women's work. It is often a cooperative enterprise that brings neighbors together. From the E. Boyd Collection, NMSRCA

Above
Arthur Rothstein shot this photo in Taos pueblo in 1936. It is taken from The American West in the Thirties: 122 Photographs by Arthur Rothstein. *Courtesy, Dover Publications*

Right
Also taken from The American West in the Thirties: 122 Photographs by Arthur Rothstein, *this photo depicts Governor Sandoval and a youngster at Taos pueblo in 1936. Courtesy, Dover Publications*

No one knows how long Indian artisans have been selling their pottery and jewelry under the portal at the Palace of the Governors, although it seems as if they have always been around. Each day hundreds of tourists carefully inspect and bargain for a wide assortment of crafts displayed by Pueblo, Navajos, and other tribes, as pictured in this photo from 1962. From the Department of Development Collection, NMSRCA

Renowned nationwide for her beautiful pottery, María Martínez (sitting at right) became one of the state's most famous artisans. The award-winning artist, a resident of the pueblo of San Ildefonso, was photographed circa 1950 with her husband Julian and an admiring tourist. From the Department of Development Collection, NMSRCA

Opposite, bottom right
Taken from The Depression Years: As Photographed by Arthur Rothstein, *this picture shows an Indian in New Mexico in 1938. Courtesy, Dover Publications*

others, was captivated by the place. New Mexico has returned the feeling, to judge by the numerous books, articles, and meetings celebrating Lawrence's New Mexico connection.

Taos continues as a significant center of American art, but Santa Fe and Albuquerque have thriving colonies as well. Even Roswell, a relatively new town on the eastern plains, has what must be one of the most remarkable museums, with a spectacular art collection, for a town its size anywhere. And the art has passed well beyond the limits of regionalism. The Southwest-based art of Georgia O'Keeffe has influenced many American artists. New Mexico studios routinely show works as exciting, and as confusing, as one could find in New York or Paris. Of course there also remains the great backbone of art more obviously sprung from New Mexico soil.

The clean, clear air of the high desert attracted others besides artists. Some people came for their health. The early decades of this century were darkened by tuberculosis, and a long stay in a sanitorium was considered the most effective cure. Many patients found the climate of New Mexico salubrious. In fact many were cured, although one doubts the 90 percent rate claimed by some at the time. And just as artists came to visit and stayed, these health-seekers stayed to make significant contributions to the state, their descendants becoming native-born New Mexicans.

Along with millions of other Americans, New Mexicans of every background were stunned as they listened to their kitchen radios and hushed the kids on December 7, 1941. The Japanese had attacked Pearl Harbor. War had come to America, and New Mexicans would be in the thick of it. The world now knows of the Navajo "Talkers," who by speaking in their native language provided a radio code that the enemy could not break. Fewer people realize that, by a quirk of fate, it was largely New Mexicans who filled the coastal antiaircraft regiments in the Philippines that fell to Japan when it captured Bataan. The Bataan Death March is remembered today in the villages and farms of New Mexico almost as a second "Long Walk" for the state. When the grim tally was in, New Mexico had suffered the highest war casualty rate, in proportion to population, of all the states in the union.

The war brought another change to New Mexico, and to the world. In mid-November of 1942 two men in an unmarked car slowly made their way up a dirt road, climbing the shoulder of a volcano. Just a million years ago this mountain had exploded incredibly, belching hundreds of cubic miles of ash and rock which then spread around its base. Eventually erosion cut steep canyons into this conglomerated "tuff," leaving long, narrow, isolated, flat-topped mesas. Atop one mesa was a private boys' school called Los Alamos. The two men—a physicist named Robert Oppenheimer and a general named Leslie Groves—got out of the car and rapidly made their decision. In the interest of the war effort they would condemn this

Top
To promote irrigation and flood control, the Federal Reclamation Service constructed Elephant Butte Dam across the Rio Grande near Hot Springs (now Truth or Consequences). The dam was the first of several major water projects within the state and was completed in 1916. From the Department of Development Collection, NMSRCA

Opposite, bottom
From the late nineteenth century up until the present, the windmill has proved to be a reliable water source for irrigation, stock water, and household use in rural areas. Rising high over the plain east of Sandía pueblo, the windmill pictured helps provide for a herd of thirsty Angus cattle. NMSRCA

Above
This 1940 photo shows the 200th regiment at summer camp near Las Vegas. From the Department of Development Collection, NMSRCA

Right
During World War II New Mexicans did their part. This circa 1942 poster encouraged Indians, Hispanos, and Anglos to buy war bonds and stamps. From the R. Vernon Hunter Collection, NMSRCA

Left
A one-room school at Versylvania is pictured in Taos in 1941. Photo by Irving Rusinow. From the Bureau of Agricultural Economics. Courtesy, National Archives

Opposite, bottom right
Unaware of the terrible struggle that lay ahead, National Guardsmen paraded the colors during 1940 summer maneuvers. From the Department of Development Collection, NMSRCA

Below
To honor the state's soldiers who fought at Bataan, the former state capitol was renamed "The Bataan Memorial Building." From the Department of Development Collection, NMSRCA

Right
On the anniversary of the bombing of Pearl Harbor, President John F. Kennedy stopped briefly in Santa Fe on December 7, 1962, only a few weeks after the Cuban missile crisis. Following a short speech the President boarded a helicopter for Los Alamos, where he was briefed concerning experiments in space rocketry. The official party included Vice-President Lyndon B. Johnson and Senator Clinton P. Anderson. MNM (#9545)

Opposite
Although there are now hundreds of other names chiseled into its soft sandstone face, El Morro has scarcely changed otherwise since 1605 when Oñate carved his inscription there. In 1906 President Theodore Roosevelt gave the area federal protection to assure its preservation. Today El Morro is a national monument. NPS

Right
Each year during the 1930s and 1940s Madrid mounted an elaborate display of Christmas lights. Although sponsored by the coal company, miners performed much of the work on their own time. In this photo an electrical holiday greeting frames the smoking breaker. From the McKittrick Collection, NMSRCA

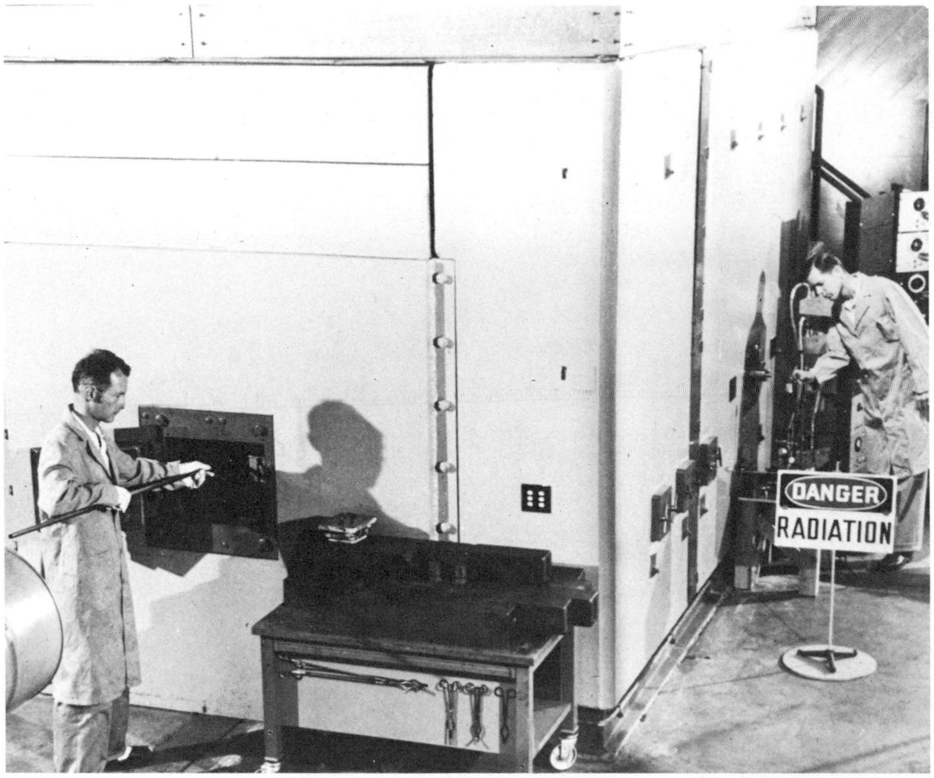

Above
Los Alamos Scientific Laboratory has led the nation in atomic research since its inception. The tools hanging in the foreground might resemble tongs from an old-fashioned blacksmith shop, but the fire in this laboratory is thousands of times hotter than any forge. From the Frank Waters Collection. Courtesy, University of New Mexico General Library, Special Collections

Right
Scientists at the laboratory are also investigating the energy potential of the geothermal regions in the nearby Jemez mountains. Courtesy, Los Alamos National Laboratory

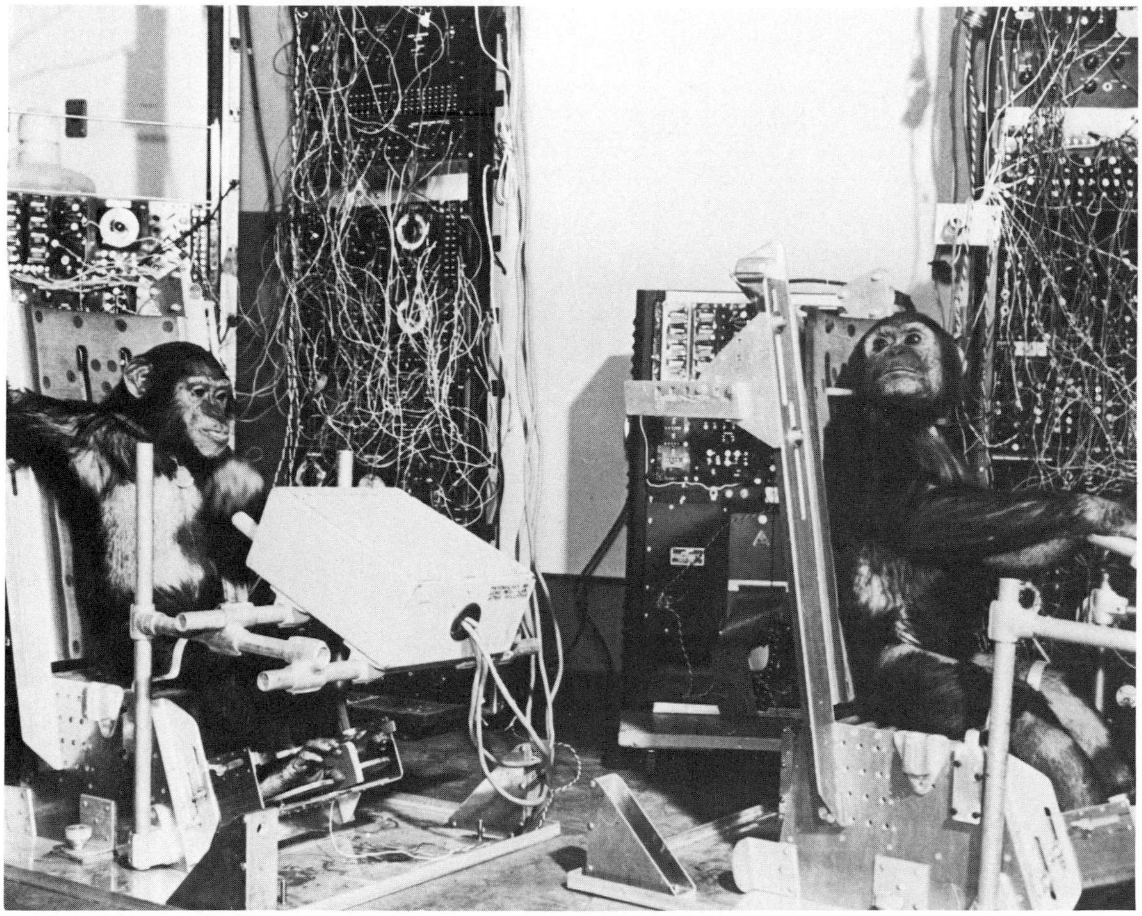

Left
In one of the most interesting experiments performed at Holloman Air Force Base, chimpanzees were used to test man's reactions to conditions in space. Space chimps Ham (left) and Enos (right), pictured circa 1961, are preparing for lift-off. On January 31, 1961, Ham became the first chimp to enter space when he rode a Redstone rocket on a transatlantic flight. From the Holloman Air Force Base Collection. Courtesy, University of New Mexico General Library, Special Collections.

Opposite, top right
As a young physics professor from Berkeley in 1922, Dr. J. Robert Oppenheimer took a pack trip over the Pajarito Plateau, the future site of Los Alamos. Twenty years later, during World War II, he was one of the scientists who selected Los Alamos Ranch School as headquarters for the top-secret Manhattan Project, which developed the atomic bomb. Oppenheimer is pictured circa 1945. From the Kittrick Collection, NMSRCA

isolated school and use the buildings for a laboratory. They were working on something of the utmost urgency and secrecy—though no one knew for certain if it was even possible. They were going to build an atomic bomb.

Working in isolation on this ridge, the team they gathered built the device in less than three years. In July 1945 they hauled it down the dirt road to an even more isolated spot about 150 miles to the south. There, at 5:30 a.m. on July 16, they tested it. The blast was stunning, of a nature never before seen on earth, and thunder rolled across the valley. New Mexico and the world had entered the atomic age.

In the forty years since World War II, New Mexico has drawn ever closer to the nation of which it is a part. The railroad, which did so much to forge the link, has been overshadowed now by the automobile and the airplane. Above all the mass media—especially network television—seem to eliminate the very idea of distance. Today New Mexicans hear their news in the same accent as does everyone else in the country. Modern movies open in Albuquerque the same week they do in Los Angeles and New York. Young people dance to the same music that their peers are listening to across the nation. A few years ago this writer watched the World Series on color television in the pueblo home of an Indian friend. (He was a Cardinals fan.)

The economy of modern New Mexico includes a mixture of farming, ranching, mining, forestry, manufacturing, and tourism. A recent addition to the list is high technology, including installations at Los Alamos, at Sandia Laboratories in Albuquerque, and at Kirtland Air Force Base. State funds have recently been directed toward fostering this type of development, creating "Centers of Excellence" in specialized technological areas at the state educational institutions. Each aims for the state-of-the-art level of research in targeted specialties like artificial intelligence and robotics. A clear advantage of such

Above
As automobiles became more popular in the years between the two world wars, state officials struggled to build a highway system to accomodate them, yet horses and mules still powered some of the road-building equipment. From the Department of Development Collection, NMSRCA

Right
In 1941 the Interstate Commerce Commission approved abandonment of the famous Chili Line, *the Denver & Rio Grande branch from Alamosa, Colorado, to Santa Fe. SHPB*

Soon after Mexico declared her independence from Spain in 1821, adventurous Missouri frontiersmen opened trade relations with New Mexico over the Santa Fe Trail. The End of the Trail, *completed by Gerald P. Cassidy in 1935, illustrated the meeting of diverse cultures that took place in Santa Fe's plaza. MNM (#6977)*

Right
American artist Seth Eastman composed this work, titled Fort Defiance at Canoncito Bonito, New Mexico, *in 1860 from a sketch by Lieutenant Colonel J.H. Eaton. Courtesy, Amon Carter Museum, Fort Worth*

Above
German artist Rudolf D.L. Cronau titled this 1885 work of his Eine Strasse in Alt-Albuquerque./Neu-Mexiko *(a street in old Albuquerque, New Mexico). Courtesy, Amon Carter Museum, Fort Worth*

Left
Design elements from this petroglyph in Galisteo Basin include simple stars, ceremonial masks, birds, and animals. They were most likely made by primitive artists some time after the fourteenth century. From the Marjorie F. Lambert Collection, NMSRCA

Left
Created from A.D. 1000-1200, Mimbres classic pottery is truly a unique art form, unmatched by any other prehistoric Southwestern pottery. The hole in the bowl pictured indicates that the vessel has been "killed," ritually, before being placed in a grave. From the Marjorie F. Lambert Collection, NMSRCA

Above
Decorations painted on the interior walls of San José Church combine Spanish- and Indian-design motifs. Pueblo symbols for sun, rain, thunder, and other elemental forces are integrated with heavy painted scrolls reminiscent of seventeenth-century Mexican church interiors. Photo by Betsy Swanson, SHPB

Left, center
The Mimbres people, a branch of the larger Mogollón prehistoric culture, made many beautiful artifacts. The turquoise frog and necklace pictured were discovered in Luna County and created between A.D. 1000-1200. From the Marjorie F. Lambert Collection, NMSRCA

Above
Bandelier National Monument is administered by the National Park Service. As an interpretative aid, the Park Service has established a self-guided tour through the ruins in Frijoles Canyon. SHPB

Right
Established after the United States conquest in 1846, Mesilla was once the economic and political center of Southern New Mexico and Arizona. The artist of this painting, titled Old Mesilla Plaza, *is unknown. MNM (#37917)*

Tucked into a beautiful mountain valley on the west slope of the Sangre de Cristo range, the pueblo of Picurís is about thirty miles south of Taos. Like Taos, Picurís belongs to the northern Tiwa linguistic group and is famous for its pottery, which is usually undecorated but glitters with bits of mica. From the Marjorie F. Lambert Collection, NMSRCA

In Pueblo Indian villages the kiva is the traditional center for community religious life. Its shape can be rectangular or round like this one at San Ildefonso. The two poles pointing skyward are part of a ladder that provides access into the building. From the Marjorie F. Lambert Collection, NMSRCA

Right
The present-day San Gerónimo Church at the pueblo of Taos replaced an earlier building destroyed in 1847 during a revolt staged by Taos Indians and Mexican nationalists against the United States conquest during the Mexican War. ACVB

Bottom, right
In 1899 one of New Mexico's most controversial murder trials took place in Hillsboro, then the seat of Sierra County. Two ranchers, Oliver Lee and Jim Gilliland, were charged with killing Henry Fountain, the eight-year-old son of Colonel Albert J. Fountain, a prominent attorney and politician from Las Cruces. The elder Fountain had been a bitter political enemy of the defense attorney, Albert B. Fall, who was suspected of master-minding the killings. Thanks to Fall's aggressive courtroom tactics, the jury found the defendants not guilty. SHPB

Bottom, left
Fort Selden, located twelve miles north of the town of Doña Ana, was established in 1865 to protect the Mesilla Valley from Apache hostilities. Recently designated a state monument, Selden's ruins have undergone extensive stabilization. SHPB

Left
New Mexico's state capitol, situated a few blocks south of Santa Fe's historic plaza, is known as the "Round House" because of its unusual shape. It is designed in a modified territorial architectural style and was completed in 1966. Photo by Panavue, ACVB

Above
El Santuario de Chimayo, erected circa 1816, is one of New Mexico's most famous religious shrines. Earth from the floor of one of its chapels is believed to have miraculous healing powers. During Holy Week, pilgrims from a wide area converge on Chimayo for Good Friday services. Photo by Panavue, ACVB

Top, right
Standing majestically on the rolling plains of eastern Colfax County, this pretentious log and sandstone residence was erected by Stephen W. Dorsey, one-time United States Senator from Arkansas. Dorsey came to New Mexico to cash in on the so-called beef bonanza of the 1870s and 1880s. Deeply involved in a national political scandal, he eventually lost his ranches. SHPB

Top
During the reoccupation of New Mexico by General Diego de Vargas in 1693 and 1694, Indians from San Ildefonso fled to Black Mesa, a natural fortress just north of their pueblo. Later other Tewas from nearby villages joined them. Together they were besieged by Spanish forces until September of 1694 when they finally agreed to surrender. From the Marjorie F. Lambert Collection, NMSRCA

Above
Federal authorities established the Gila Wilderness Area in 1924. The Gila comprised 750,000 unspoiled acres, the first lands in the nation to receive wilderness designation. The wilderness is pictured circa 1975. ACVB

Right
The yucca blossom is New Mexico's state flower. The yucca was originally selected by New Mexican school children and their choice was officially confirmed by the legislature in 1927. ACVB

Flanked by the San Andres Mountains on the west and the Sacramentos to the east, White Sands National Monument lies in South-Central New Mexico's Tulurosa Basin. For centuries snow and rain water from the two high ranges have eroded the gypsum deposits below, creating huge wave-like dunes of dazzling white sand. The area became a national monument in 1933. ACVB

Although New Mexico is typically an arid land with a scanty amount of rainfall, a few well-timed summer showers can change a barren plain into a desert flower garden almost overnight, as shown in this 1950 photograph. Photo by Nat Dodge, NPS

Below
The spectacular Cloudcroft trestle, situated on the Alamagordo and Sacramento Mountain Railroad, was erected in 1890 to span Mexican Canyon. Promoters built the A & SM to haul timber out of the mountains and carry tourists to an ornate resort hotel at Cloudcroft. Economic conditions forced abandonment of the line in 1947. The Cloudcroft trestle is pictured in 1981. Photo by Betsy Swan, SHPB

Right
Soon after the first frost touches the state's mountain ranges, the aspen foliage turns from green to a brilliant gold. Every fall scores of motorists head for the hills to experience the dramatic color change. Others ride the Cumbres and Toltec Scenic Railway from Chama to Antonito, Colorado, passing through a particularly spectacular area. Courtesy, Ludwig and Laino

Left
After a short struggle, General Diego de Vargas recaptured Santa Fe from Pueblo Indian rebels in December of 1693. Each year his triumphant reentry into the city is acted out during Santa Fe's fiesta. Courtesy, Ludwig and Laino

Bottom, left
To commemorate the recapture of Santa Fe by General Diego de Vargas in 1693, the small statue of "La Conquistadora" is carried in procession each year from Saint Francis Cathedral to Rosario Chapel. The chapel was erected in 1806 and stands on the site where Vargas camped while besieging the city. Courtesy, Ludwig and Laino

Bottom, right
Chile is an important crop in New Mexico and a vital part of the local cuisine. Aficionados disagree as to whether the most potent chile comes from the northern or southern parts of the state, but both are said to be hot! Photo by Betsy Swanson, SHPB

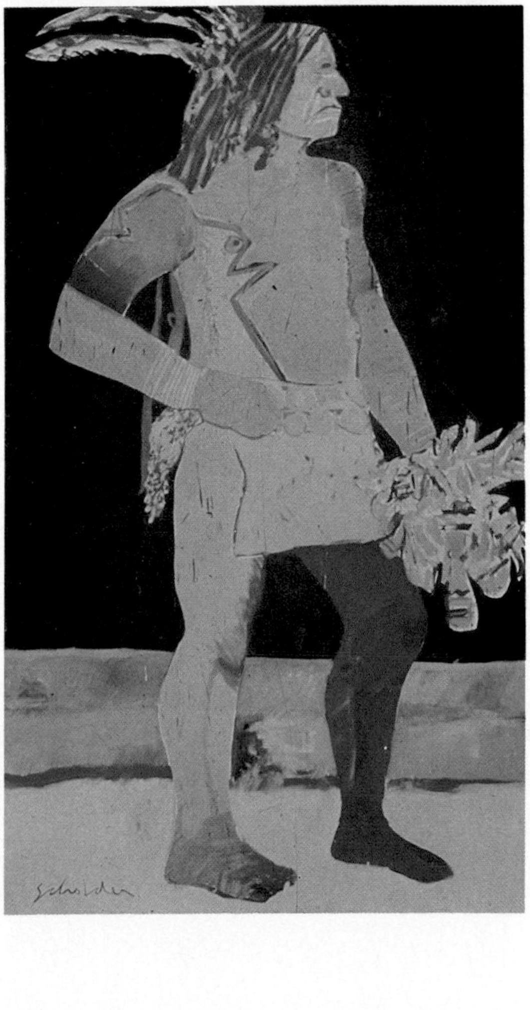

Left
Leon Kroll came to New Mexico for a brief stay in the summer of 1917. While visiting his friends Robert Henri and George Bellows, both well-known Eastern artists, Kroll painted The Hills of Santa Fe, *pictured here. MNM (#45495)*

Opposite
Velino Herrera created this vivid watercolor, Pueblo Mother, *in 1939. Herrera, born in 1902 in Zia pueblo, started painting at the age of fifteen and later adopted the nickname Ma-Pe Wi. Courtesy, Amon Carter Museum, Fort Worth*

Bottom, left
Gustave Baumann, one of New Mexico's most popular artists, is best known for his woodblock prints depicting trees, flowers, and mountain scenery near Santa Fe and Taos. The view from the road leading into Ranchos de Taos plaza is shown in this print. Courtesy, Fine Arts Museum, MNM

Bottom, right
Fritz Scholder is a New Mexico artist with a national reputation who frequently incorporated contemporary Indian themes into his early work. Because of their social content his paintings and lithographs struck a responsive chord during the Native American protest movement of the 1960s and 1970s. Courtesy, Fine Arts Museum, MNM

Above
Albuquerque claims the title of Hot Air Balloon Capital of the World. *Every fall enthusiasts come from near and far to take part in an annual balloon fiesta. The event began in 1972 when a local pilot made a balloon excursion the focus of his mother's birthday party. ACVB*

Livestock production continues to be one of New Mexico's most important industries. The herd of Charolais and Hereford cattle pictured is headed for summer pasture in the high country. ACVB

Energy shortages have drawn attention to the coal supplies found in the Southwest. Deposits are exploited by huge mechanical shovels working night and day, as in this strip mine near Farmington. Photo by Fred Mang, Jr., NPS

May through October is rodeo time in New Mexico. Each year both professional and amateur contests attract large crowds of enthusiastic fans from throughout the state. This bareback bronc rider spurred high over his horse's shoulders hoping to receive a winning score from the judges at the Rodeo de Santa Fe. Courtesy, Ludwig and Laino

The Four Corners Generating Plant at Farmington is fired by coal from nearby strip mines and was constructed by a consortium of utility companies at a cost of $168 million. The plant provides electricity for a wide area in the Southwest, but the pollution that it creates is a chronic environmental problem. Photo by Fred Mang, Jr., NPS

Located five miles northeast of Albuquerque, the Sandia Peak aerial tramway is the longest in North America and third longest in the world. It rises up the rugged west face of the Sandias from 6,600 feet to 10,378 feet at the crest, a distance of 2.7 miles, in twenty minutes. Views from the top are spectacular. Photo by Panavue, ACVB

In the 1940s skiing became a popular sport in New Mexico. Attracted by the region's bright winter sunshine and lighter-than-air powder snow, skiers came to the Southwest from all over the nation. In an era of laced leather boots and wooden skis, this chairlift was a remarkable innovation. These pioneer skiers posed for a picture at the Santa Fe Ski Basin circa 1947. From the Department of Development Collection, NMSRCA

Situated on the Colorado-New Mexico border, Raton Pass presented a formidable obstacle to nineteenth-century railroad engineers seeking a feasible route into the territory. This view looks over the present city of Raton to the distant mesas and plains beyond. From the Department of Development Collection, NMSRCA

Above
The Santa Fe Opera presented its first performance July 3, 1957, in a brand-new outdoor theater five miles north of the city. Success marked the opera's early years, but the original building was destroyed by fire during July of 1967 in the midst of the summer season. Undismayed, opera founder and general manager John O. Crosby completed the season in a downtown school gymnasium. The reconstructed opera house is pictured in 1977. Photo by David Stein. Courtesy, Santa Fe Opera

Right
The Santa Fe Opera's 1983 season opened with a dazzling production of Jacques Offenbach's Orpheus in the Underworld, *a satire of the Olympian gods. Shown in this 1983 picture are bass-baritone Claude Corbeil as Jupiter and mezzo-soprano Judith Christin as Juno. Photo by Michael Blumenthal. Courtesy, Santa Fe Opera*

scientific and technical endeavors is that they are relatively unaffected by vast distances and lack of water—New Mexico's traditional conditions. And the stunning beauty of the land and the fascination of its cultures are as attractive to scientists as to all others who have come to the state to stay.

For it may be here that one finds the true, abiding wealth of New Mexico. The mesas in the evening sun are as beautiful today as in centuries past, and as long as the tricultural mix can avoid becoming too homogenized, it will continue to enrich the lives of residents and visitors alike. There is some combination here, of space and color and light, of challenge and occasional reward, that is as attractive to modern technological man as it was to the Pueblos who loved it first. It was they who first dug turquoise from the earth, a stone that is worn today by New Mexicans of every culture. Some say the stone is a piece of the New Mexican sky. If that is so, one could do worse than to wear it wherever he goes.

Albuquerque, founded in 1706, is New Mexico's largest city, with a population of about 455,000 living in the metropolitan area. The city was named for the Duke of Alburquerque, viceroy of New Spain. The first "r" in the spelling was dropped. Photo by Dick Kent. ACVB

Although present-day lumberjacks prefer chainsaws to double-bitted axes, timber producers continue to provide building material that sustains the state's urban growth. Unfortunately a recent nationwide slump in housing starts has had a negative impact on New Mexico's lumber industry. From the Department of Development Collection, NMSRCA

Partners in Progress

From stone age to space age, the history of business in New Mexico is a fascinating story. Long before Spanish conquistadores appeared on the Rio Grande in the sixteenth century, indigenous Indian tribes carried on an active trade in agricultural products, pottery, salt, dried meat, and turquoise. Other items unavailable locally, such as shells and exotic feathers for ceremonial purposes, were exchanged over great distances from one village to the next.

After Juan de Oñate founded New Mexico's first permanent colony in 1598, his followers depended mainly on subsistence farming for support. Lacking industry and mineral resources, the settlement produced few marketable commodities which caused a woeful balance of payments with New Spain. Besides sheep and woolen products, the colonists exported goods obtained from Indian neighbors. In return for their hides, skins, and coarse textiles, the natives received horses, metal tools, and weapons, innovations that brought profound changes to Indian cultures.

Because Spanish colonial policy mandated imprisonment for intruders, business relations with foreigners were almost nonexistent. That situation changed rapidly following Mexican independence, however. In 1821 William Becknell opened the Santa Fe Trail, the great commercial highway from Missouri to New Mexico. Besides providing local residents with a wondrous array of merchandise, the trail established contacts between New Mexicans and Anglo-Americans that prepared the way for United States conquest during the Mexican War.

When hostilities ended, the military presence in New Mexico caused a brief boom since Army payrolls and supply contracts greatly increased the amount of cash in circulation. Anglo entrepreneurs established new industries and began prospecting for precious metals despite Indian hostilities. In the towns, banks, newspapers, hotels, and other service industries sprang up.

New Mexico remained remote, however, until the railroad pushed over Raton Pass in 1878, integrating the territory into the national economy. Trains not only provided markets for livestock and minerals but also brought a throng of immigrants who introduced eastern ideas and fashions. Irrigation projects and other technological departures led to expansion in agriculture at the turn of the century. After World War I the discovery of important oil and gas reserves caused rapid development in the state's northwest and southeast corners.

World War II stimulated a new wave of economic growth. Frequently, servicemen stationed within the state decided to remain after discharge. Development of the atomic bomb at Los Alamos gave an advantage in securing peacetime nuclear energy and aerospace projects. More recently, the national migration to the Sun Belt has caused another population surge. Attracted by the climate and a pool of skilled personnel, many high-technology companies have established themselves within the state.

The organizations whose stories are detailed on the following pages have chosen to support this important literary and civic project. They illustrate the variety of ways in which individuals and their businesses have contributed to the growth and development of the state. The civic involvement of New Mexico's businesses, institutions of learning, and government, in cooperation with its citizens, has made the state an excellent place to live and work.

CHAPTER VIII

HISTORICAL SOCIETY OF NEW MEXICO

On December 26, 1859, a group of prominent New Mexicans, both Hispanic and Anglo, gathered at the Palace of the Governors in Santa Fe to organize the Historical Society of New Mexico. Founding members included Army officers, attorneys, churchmen, politicians, and merchants. Once assembled, they adopted a constitution and elected Colonel John B. Grayson as president. For more than a year the membership carried on an active program, holding monthly meetings with speakers on historical subjects. The Society also began collecting artifacts and historical documents. Unfortunately, the Civil War ended the group's activities after president Grayson and other members cast their lot with the Confederacy and left New Mexico.

On the twenty-first anniversary of the original organization, a number of old members and other interested persons met in December 1880 to reestablish the Society. William G. Ritch, Secretary of the Territory, was chosen president. Several years later the Society obtained use of rooms in the Palace when most territorial officials moved to the new capitol, completed in 1885.

In 1909 the territorial legislature turned over the Palace of the Governors to the newly created Museum of New Mexico. The building also became the headquarters of the School of American Archaeology, a private institution now known as the School of American Research.

Dr. Edgar Lee Hewett served as director of both the museum and the school. The Society retained its rooms in the Palace, however, and for the next fifty years the affairs of the three institutions became hopelessly intertwined. Meanwhile, in 1927 the legislature attempted to control the increasing accumulation of records created by state agencies by making the Society custodian of the public archives. Subsequently, legislators made appropriations to the Society for records management purposes but entrusted administration of the funds to the museum, an arrangement that proved unworkable.

William G. Ritch, Secretary of the Territory, was chosen president of the Historical Society of New Mexico in 1880. Courtesy, Museum of New Mexico (Neg. no. 10759)

Recognizing that the interlocking relationship between the three institutions could not continue, officials took legal action to resolve the problem. In 1959 the legislature ordered separation of the Museum of New Mexico and the School of American Research. The lawmakers also established a new agency, the State Records Center, with responsibility for the public archives, repealing the 1927 act that had made the Society official custodian.

As a result, the Historical Society of New Mexico reincorporated as a private body with no ties to the museum or other state agencies. Interest in the organization lagged for some years, but in 1973 a group of zealous members started a revitalization. Two years later the membership adopted a new constitution and began planning a professional conference that is now held annually at various locations across the state. Presently the Society has 500 members and sponsors a wide range of activities in the historical field.

The Society's room, in the Palace of Governors in Santa Fe, circa 1910. Courtesy, Museum of New Mexico (Neg. no. 6763)

BARKER REALTY, INC.

Barker Realty, Inc., was founded by Laughlin Barker in 1974. A decade earlier Barker had returned to Santa Fe to begin a new career after twenty-five years of active duty with the U.S. Navy. Lacking in industry, the capital city seemed to offer few opportunities at that time but Barker thought that the real estate business would have some potential. Twenty years of experience have proved his foresight well justified. Today Barker Realty, Inc., is a diversified real estate company dealing in residential and commercial property. In addition, Barker Management Corp. also manages the Barker family's extensive downtown holdings and other commercial properties.

Barker's father, William J. Barker, came to Santa Fe in 1912 as a young lawyer fresh out of George Washington University Law School. Soon after his arrival he joined a law firm headed by N.B. Laughlin, one of New Mexico's most prominent attorneys. A powerful figure in Democratic politics, Laughlin also invested in downtown real estate.

Within a few years young William J. Barker married Ruth Laughlin, daughter of the firm's senior partner. A professional author, Ruth Laughlin Barker wrote two books: *Caballeros* and *The Wind Leaves No Shadow*, a historical novel concerning Santa Fe at the time of its occupation by United States forces in 1846. First published in 1948, this book has remained popular and is still in print.

As a boy, Laughlin Barker was crazy about flying. His fascination began in 1927, when Charles Lindbergh stopped briefly in Santa Fe soon after his epic transatlantic flight. A few years later Barker decided to make aviation part of his life following a short ride in a Ford Trimotor then touring New Mexico.

In 1939 he received an appointment to the U.S. Naval Academy at Annapolis, graduating in the midst of World War II. After two years in the South Pacific combat zone, he shifted to aviation, becoming a carrier pilot. With peace restored, Barker flew from carriers in the Mediterranean and Western Pacific theaters. Later he served as a planner for U. S. Sixth Fleet-NATO exercises. After several years at the Pentagon under the Chief of Naval Operations, he retired in 1964 with the rank of commander.

Located at the corner of Don Gaspar Avenue and San Francisco Street, the Laughlin Building is Barker's largest downtown property. Now remodeled in Spanish Territorial architectural style, it was erected in 1906 by N.B. Laughlin who maintained his law offices on the second floor. Courtesy, Museum of New Mexico

A civilian once more, Barker came home and went to work as a salesman for Bishop, Manuel and Hunker, a leading Santa Fe real estate firm. As his capability increased, Barker also became an appraiser for Mutual Building and Loan, an important local lender. In 1974 he established his own company, Barker Realty, Inc. Five years later his son David Barker joined the company. Despite many business activities, Laughlin Barker participated in a variety of civic organizations, serving as chairman of the board of trustees for St. Vincent's Hospital, the United Fund, and president of the Chamber of Commerce. He also was a founder and is a director of the Sunwest Bank of Santa Fe.

COLLEGE OF SANTA FE

Most of the old Army buildings that made up the original College of Santa Fe campus have been replaced with permanent structures. The Fogelson Library (shown here) was dedicated in 1970.

Although the College of Santa Fe has been located at its present site for less than forty years, its roots go back to the mid-nineteenth century. In 1859 four members of the Brothers of Christian Schools arrived in Santa Fe from France to establish a school for boys. Known as St. Michael's College, the new institution was part of a major effort made by Jean Baptiste Lamy, New Mexico's famous Roman Catholic bishop, to improve educational opportunities in his diocese. When classes began the Brothers had only an adobe hut for a schoolroom, but enrollment climbed quickly to 180 students in spite of the crude facilities. At first the curriculum included a mix of high school and college courses.

During the next decades the school continued to grow. In 1874 St. Michael's became the first institution in New Mexico authorized to confer degrees under terms of an act of incorporation passed by the Territorial Legislature. Four years later the school moved into a new three-story adobe building next to San Miguel Chapel a few blocks south of Santa Fe's plaza.

For the next seventy years St. Michael's endeavored to meet the educational requirements of northern New Mexico, stressing the needs of the large Hispanic population. At the end of World War II the Christian Brothers, under the leadership of Brother Benildus, obtained a location on Santa Fe's south side to open a newly organized four-year college; the old downtown campus remained the high school campus. The new site included 124 acres of land and forty-two frame buildings, part of the former Bruns General Hospital which had been declared surplus by the War Assets Administration. Once again, the Brothers faced a challenging task.

Directed by a new president, Brother Cyprian Luke, an extensive fund raising in 1958 succeeded so well that school officials were able to dedicate a new lecture hall within three years. Other new buildings soon followed, including a spacious theater and an impressive library, named for actress Greer Garson and her husband, E.E. Fogelson, who have been generous donors to the college. In 1966 the institution adopted its present name, College of Santa Fe.

Today the college has an enrollment of 850 students representing all parts of the nation although the majority are from northern New Mexico. The present course of study emphasizes the humanities, mathematics and science, business, nursing, and the performing arts.

In July 1982 Brother Donald Mouton was elected president by the College of Santa Fe board of trustees.

Each year the college's Performing Arts Department stages several theatrical productions, sometimes featuring guest artists. Flanked by students, Greer Garson is pictured above during a rehearsal of Jean Girandoux's Madwoman of Chaillot. *Photo by Les Raschko, 1975*

LA FONDA

One of the Southwest's great hotels, La Fonda, stands on a corner of Santa Fe's famous plaza at the end of the Santa Fe Trail. Although La Fonda is a mere sixty-five years old, the site has provided lodging facilities for 300 years and is part of the city's romantic heritage. In 1848, less than two years after the United States conquest of New Mexico, an enterprising businessman named John C. Moody opened a hostelry called the Independence House on the same location. One of several competing hotels in the capital city, Independence House welcomed a wide variety of frontier travelers including Army officers, politicians, gamblers, merchants, and clergymen. Subsequently, Moody's establishment changed hands, was enlarged, and became the Exchange Hotel, but bilingual patrons usually called it "la fonda" (the inn).

The Exchange fell on hard times after serving as a regional social center for several decades, but even its demise had a certain flair. As part of a Liberty Bond rally after World War I, patriotic citizens razed the building with an Army tank, crashing into the walls following each sale of a $100 bond. To nurture the budding tourist industry, city fathers solicited funds for a new hotel, La Fonda, at the same site. Unfortunately, the project foundered when capital raised from community stock subscriptions proved inadequate. After long negotiations the local promoters in 1926 sold La Fonda to Santa Fe Land and Improvement Company, a subsidiary of the Santa Fe Railroad. Once in control, railroad officials leased La Fonda to Fred Harvey, the famous managerial firm then operating tourist hotels and related enterprises throughout the Southwest. In planning the decor, Harvey personnel brought in Mary Colter, an experienced designer who gave La Fonda its distinctive character.

Sometimes known as "The Inn at the End of the Trail," La Fonda stands at the southeast corner of Santa Fe's historic plaza.

Under Harvey's management, La Fonda became known throughout the world as the place to stay in Santa Fe. In the 1960s, however, industry leaders lost confidence in older, downtown hotels. As a result, railroad executives quickly accepted an offer to purchase La Fonda from a group of investors headed by Samuel B. Ballen, a Dallas oil man who had recently moved to Santa Fe. Although Ballen and his associates lacked hotel experience, they had great faith in the city. By preserving La Fonda's unique charm they hoped to strengthen Santa Fe's historic downtown and prevent urban decay.

Known as Corporación de la Fonda, the new ownership took over in 1968 and immediately began a comprehensive improvement program that has continued to the present. In addition to replacing the building's plumbing and climate-control systems, the corporation has enlarged the bar, rearranged the lobby, and redecorated all the guest rooms, reproducing much of the original Colter-designed furniture. Current plans include a three-level carriage house topped by a roof garden landscaped with native plants and shrubs, part of the effort to maintain La Fonda as one of Santa Fe's most enduring landmarks.

In the 1930s a mariachi band serenaded La Fonda's guests as they relaxed after a day of sightseeing.

THE NEW MEXICAN

The New Mexican*'s front door faces on Marcy Street.*

Founded as a weekly in 1849 by E.T. Davies and W.E. Jones, the Santa Fe *New Mexican* is the Southwest's oldest newspaper. No stranger to controversy, the paper has expounded a wide range of editorial opinions during its 135-year history. When the first issue came off the press on November 28, it consisted of four pages, two in English, two in Spanish. The subscription price was seven dollars per year. The new journal succeeded an earlier English-language sheet, the Santa Fe *Republican,* which Davies had published in 1847, using a United States Army press manned by soldiers. Anxious to end this arrangement, the military sold the plant to Davies and Jones when they established *The New Mexican.* Like many frontier journals, the paper came out sporadically in its first years. Dependent on monthly mail service for outside news, the editor relied heavily on local events to fill his pages, padding any gaps with prolonged serial stories and humorous material. Political rivalries, Indian raids, murders, and natural disasters received heavy emphasis.

In November 1863 *The New Mexican* was purchased by one of its employees, William H. Manderfield, an experienced printer from Pennsylvania who had hired on as shop foreman during the Civil War. Six months later Manderfield formed a partnership with Thomas S. Tucker. Together they made *The New Mexican* into a leading regional newspaper despite delinquent subscribers and an untrained work force. In those years the paper combined a boundless faith in New Mexico's future with uncompromising political partisanship. Feature articles lauded Republican candidates, promoted construction of a transcontinental railroad, and criticized government Indian policy. Editorially *The New Mexican* also championed the Union and free public schools. In 1868 the paper became a daily.

After almost a decade of ups and downs, the *Daily New Mexican* fell on hard times in 1877, forcing Manderfield and Tucker to suspend publication for a time. Two years later the operating company reorganized and the paper revived, thanks to new capital supplied by the Atchison, Topeka, and Santa Fe Railroad, which had recently extended its tracks into the territory. During the next few decades *The New Mexican* changed hands several times, causing its political affiliation to change as well. Despite factional seesawing, the paper continued steadfast support for New Mexico's efforts to become a state, the predominant issue of the era.

Coincidentally, within a few

Ed Brown works on The New Mexican'*s presses.*

months after New Mexico achieved statehood early in 1912, *The New Mexican* had been sold again. The new owner was Bronson M. Cutting, a New Yorker who had come west for his health. A political ally of Theodore Roosevelt and other Progressives, Cutting had been educated at Groton and Harvard. At first glance his aristocratic background made him seem out of place in the West, but he quickly established himself as a powerful and ruthless politician. To direct *The New Mexican,* Cutting chose as his editor E. Dana Johnson, an extremely capable journalist. Johnson made the paper lively and exciting despite an obvious political bias.

Intensely ambitious, Cutting used *The New Mexican* to publicize Progressive causes and promote his own political advancement. In 1927 Governor Richard C. Dillon named Cutting to the United States Senate following the death of incumbent A.A. Jones. After a successful campaign to regain the seat seven years later, Cutting died suddenly in an airplane crash in Missouri, thus ending a long and colorful career.

In the wake of Cutting's death, *The New Mexican* again experienced various changes of ownership before its purchase by Robert M. McKinney in 1948, just prior to the paper's 100th birthday. The son of a Texas minister, McKinney learned the newspaper trade working on Amarillo dailies. Fortunately the new owner retained the previous editor, Will Harrison, who had lived in Santa Fe long enough to love the town and understand its eccentricities. In addition to editorials, Harrison also wrote a popular column entitled "Inside the Capitol." Other columnists of that period included such well-known local personalities as Oliver La Farge and Will Shuster. To emphasize Santa Fe's special qualities as an artistic and literary center, Harrison set up a Sunday supplement devoted to local cultural activities.

Features editor Ron Fransell (left) and assistant managing editor Dan Hogan work at The New Mexican'*s copy desk.*

In 1976, after directing *The New Mexican* for almost thirty years, McKinney sold the paper to its present owner, the Gannett Company, Inc., of Rochester, New York. In return he received a large block of Gannett stock. From a modest beginning as a family-owned newspaper in Elmira, New York, Gannett has grown into a media conglomerate now operating eighty-seven newspapers; seven television and radio stations; *USA Today,* a national newspaper; and several advertising subsidiaries in the United States and Canada. The purchase agreement stipulated that McKinney would remain active in the paper's management and retain the titles of publisher and editor-in-chief.

On August 27, 1984, under the management of Wayne C. Vann, president, *The New Mexican* successfully converted from weekday evening delivery to morning, culminating more than a year of planning and surveys.

Santa Feans woke up to a much expanded news product including a full stock market report which had been impossible under the evening delivery schedule. Weather coverage was expanded, as was local, national, and world news coverage.

With the guaranteed 6:30 a.m. delivery, subscribers responded well, adding to home delivery as well as street sales circulation figures immediately. The move to mornings allowed *The New Mexican* to continue to maintain its traditional position as one of the state's most influential newspapers and to continue to serve the needs of readers in the expanding market of northern New Mexico.

RANCHO ENCANTADO

Surrounded by piñon and juniper trees, Rancho Encantado is situated at the foot of the towering Sangre de Cristo Mountains eight miles north of Santa Fe.

From its inception in 1968 Rancho Encantado has been a family enterprise conducted by Betty Egan and her children. Following the death of her husband, Mrs. Egan, her son, and two daughters left their home in Cleveland, Ohio, hoping to find the right place to start a new life in the Southwest. Although they had no specific goal at first, the Egans believed that a guest ranch might provide some interesting opportunities.

After three summers and many miles of travel through Texas, Arizona, Colorado, and New Mexico, Betty Egan finally found the perfect location at Rancho del Monte, a deteriorating dude ranch in the foothills of the Sangre de Cristo Mountains eight miles north of Santa Fe. In the 1950s the ranch had belonged to Bill and Barbara Hooten, who described their experiences as hosts to the public in the best-seller *Guestward Ho!* The property had fallen on bad times, however, and required extensive renovation when Betty Egan bought it in 1967.

To help with the multitude of necessary repairs and alterations, both John and Veronica Egan left college. Betsy Egan, then thirteen, assumed responsibility for the household, buying groceries and cooking meals. Unfortunately, their plans suffered a severe setback when Betty Egan became ill in the midst of the remodeling. Son John stepped into the breach, however, and provided the leadership to get the construction program back on schedule. During his mother's convalescence, it was agreed that John would become the ranch's general manager. John now holds the title of owner/manager.

After confronting all the usual problems as well as many unexpected ones, the contractors completed the renovation and Rancho Encantado opened for business with a gala reception in July 1968. Translated from Spanish, the name means "Enchanted Ranch." For the Egans its completion was a dream come true. From the beginning Betty Egan has assured the comfort of her guests by operating the ranch as though it were her own home. More luxurious than most guest ranches but less pretentious than the usual resort hotel, Rancho Encantado is an unusual blend of features from both. Through the years a host of notables from politics and show business have signed the ranch register, including Senator Jacob Javits, Nelson Rockefeller, Maria Callas, Robert Redford, Prince Rainier and Princess Grace of Monaco, and Princess Anne of Great Britain.

Recently the Egans began a real estate venture on a site adjoining resort headquarters. Known as Pueblo Encantado, the development consists of a cluster of condominiums nestled into the foothills of the Sangre de Cristos. Carefully designed to ensure compatibility with the land, the new units are intended for those desiring a place of their own next to the Enchanted Ranch.

NEW MEXICO BLUE CROSS AND BLUE SHIELD, INC.

Concern over medical bills became pronounced in the late 1920s. In response, prepaid health programs, now known as Blue Cross and Blue Shield Plans, developed throughout the nation. For millions of Americans, the Blue Cross and Blue Shield name means financial security to provide protection against the high cost of health care. New Mexico Blue Cross and Blue Shield is one of ninety-six Blue Cross and Blue Shield Plans, which together finance health care for over eighty million people.

In 1940 a group of health professionals in Albuquerque established a hospital prepayment plan known as Hospital Service, Inc. Nine months after its incorporation the new plan had obtained 130 subscriptions covering 240 people. It had one member facility, Presbyterian Hospital, in Albuquerque. Within two years membership had climbed to 1,100, and another Albuquerque hospital, St. Joseph, had joined Presbyterian as a participating institution. Subscribers paid monthly fees of seventy-five cents for individuals and two dollars for families. Hospitals were paid approximately six dollars per day for care. By 1945 the plan had been accepted by additional hospitals in Santa Fe, Las Vegas, and Raton. During that same year Hospital Service officially became a Blue Cross Plan and part of the national organization. In 1946 the forerunner to New Mexico Blue Shield was developed to pay for physician services. During the next several years both organizations grew and became health-care financers statewide. Operating as separate, but coordinated organizations, the two corporations merged in 1972 to become New Mexico Blue Cross and Blue Shield, Inc.

Today New Mexico Blue Cross and Blue Shield provides health coverage to over 200,000 New Mexicans. It is also the Medicare intermediary and performs financial services for the state's Medicaid program. The corporation paid over $250 million in health benefits in 1983. It has a board of directors comprised of twenty-five New Mexico citizens for all parts of the state. It is also one of the state's leading employers, with 325 employees. The largest office is located in Albuquerque and there are six other offices throughout New Mexico.

The corporation offers a full range of health financing and life insurance packages. It provides flexible benefit and financing services to employers, as well as comprehensive data and management capabilities. Once an organization that focused primarily on providing access to health care, it now works closely with employers to assure the reasonable management of access to and purchasing of hospital and medical services.

Through its unique relationship with providers of health care, New Mexico Blue Cross and Blue Shield is committed to offering access to medical services at affordable prices to large and small employer groups and to individual consumers as well.

BIG JO LUMBER COMPANY

The Big Jo Lumber Company at its old location on Santa Fe's San Francisco Street. The store's sign appealed to its bilingual clientele.

Big Jo's new owners are Richard C de Baca and his sons, Ronald (left) and Richard Jr. (right).

Big Jo Hardware Company is one of Santa Fe's newest businesses but, despite its recent origin, it has a long tradition in the community. To explain this paradox, it is necessary to go back to 1927 when Ferdinand A. Berry decided to move to Santa Fe. His employer, Big Jo Lumber Company of Liberal, Kansas, operated yards in eastern New Mexico at Artesia, Roswell, and Clayton. During his travels Berry had visited Santa Fe and decided it would be a good place to raise a family. After some investigation, he purchased Santa Fe Mill and Lumber Co. from Frank N. Thompson and established a branch of Big Jo in the capital city.

Beginning with a storefront on San Francisco Street, Berry expanded until his yard covered most of the block. In the 1950s Berry's two daughters, Marie and Perle, and their husbands, Robert A. Santheson and John D. Hillyer, Jr., became increasingly active in management, eventually assuming ownership. Together they ran Big Jo as an old fashioned lumberyard. Customers included contractors, ranchers, and "do-it-yourself" enthusiasts from throughout northern New Mexico.

Early in 1983 the Santhesons and Hillyers sold their prime downtown location to El Dorado Partnership. When news of the sale became public, many Santa Feans feared they had seen the last of the old firm which had become a landmark on lower San Francisco Street. In September, however, a buyer came forward, purchased the Big Jo store's inventory, and moved everything to a location on Siler Road on Santa Fe's south side. The new owners, Richard C de Baca and his sons, Ronald and Richard Jr., adopted the name Big Jo Hardware Company when they opened for business.

A former chief of the New Mexico State Police, the elder C de Baca had recently retired after twenty-seven years of service. Beginning as a raw recruit, he had risen through the ranks and had been named head of the agency in 1982 by former Governor Bruce King. Although he had no background in merchandising, both of C de Baca's sons had had experience with building supply firms in Santa Fe and Las Cruces. Well established at their new site, the C de Bacas continue to use the Big Jo logo, a gigantic lumberjack carrying a big double-bitted ax, the symbol that has characterized the company for almost sixty years.

Richard C de Baca and his sons intend to continue to provide contractors and "do-it-yourselfers" with quality merchandise and friendly, personal service.

Big Jo Hardware as it now appears at its new location on Siler Road.

THE PETERS CORPORATION

Recently acquired by The Peters Corporation, the site of Sena Plaza once belonged to Captain Diego Arias de Quiros, who served under General Diego de Vargas during the reoccupation of New Mexico in 1698.

Jerry Peters first began to buy and sell western fine art on a small scale while still in college. Today The Peters Corporation has grown to include a real estate firm, a construction company, a publishing house, and a restaurant, in addition to owning one of the finest art galleries in the Southwest. It has become one of Santa Fe's fastest-growing businesses, and for the past decade its growth has paralleled that of the city itself.

A native of Denver, Peters first came to Santa Fe as a student at St. John's College where he developed a lively interest in fine art. Between classes he frequented local museums and galleries and educated himself in the schools of southwestern painting. Lacking capital at first, he confined himself to selling works consigned by other collectors. As his proficiency increased, he handled drawings and small paintings while also assembling the nucleus of his own collection.

Peters moved the gallery from his home to a rambling adobe on Camino del Monte Sol built by Mary Hunter Austin, a prominent author of the 1920s. Although he continues to show the classic western artists and the Taos founders, he has recently featured other schools as well, including the American and French Impressionists and New Mexico's own Georgia O'Keeffe. In order to provide catalogs for his exhibitions, he established a publishing subsidiary which has brought forth definitive volumes that combine interpretive and biographical essays with a selection of the artists' work.

With his gallery running successfully, Jerry Peters has turned his attention to other ventures. For several years he renovated old adobe homes, later shifting to downtown commercial properties. In 1981 he acquired one of Santa Fe's most historic landmarks, Sena Plaza, a complex of galleries, shops, and offices now undergoing extensive restoration including the reopening of a restaurant housed there in the 1920s. La Casa Sena offers a variety of New Mexican and Continental cuisine both indoors and in the plaza's garden. The cantina features singing and music from Broadway shows and light opera.

More recently Peters has bought several additional buildings in the heart of the city, where he has continued renovation work. Plaza Mercado on old San Francisco Street features a three-story glass atrium running through all three levels, with both office and retail spaces. Peters has integrated a construction firm with his real estate interests in order to maintain a full-time crew of craftsmen specializing in New Mexican building techniques.

Located in a rambling adobe building on Santa Fe's east side, The Peters Gallery exhibits one of the nation's finest collections of western fine art.

ST. JOHN'S COLLEGE

Situated in the foothills of the Sangre de Cristo Mountains on Santa Fe's east side, St. John's College is small, coeducational, and devoted to the liberal arts. St. John's is an independent institution with no religious or political affiliation. The school's avowed objective is deceptively simple—teaching young men and women how to learn together and enjoy the excellent accomplishments of our culture. To achieve that goal St. John's has adopted an unusual curriculum focused on the study of over 130 books, each one a landmark in Western culture. Ranging from Plato and Homer to Darwin and Freud, the authors also include St. Augustine, Sir Isaac Newton, Shakespeare, Karl Marx, and Einstein. By concentrating on these monumental works, the college seeks to imbue its students with the fundamentals of Western literature, philosophy, history, mathematics, and the natural sciences. At St. John's there are no departments and no majors. All undergraduates follow the same course of study which leads to a bachelor of arts degree.

Although St. John's Santa Fe campus is relatively new, the college originated at Annapolis, Maryland, soon after the American Revolution. In 1784 the Maryland State Legislature chartered St. John's College as an institution to which "youth of all religious denominations shall be freely and liberally admitted... according to their merit." To supervise administration the legislature established a board of visitors and governors, a body that has exercised oversight ever since. During its early years the school remained small, offering a solid, traditional education to its students. In 1937 St. John's adopted the so-called "Great Books" curriculum, a program that had grown from the deliberations of the Committee on Liberal Arts, a group of nationally known scholars appointed by Robert Maynard Hutchins who was president of the University of Chicago. Their plan aroused widespread interest among educators and resulted in a growing enrollment at St. John's.

St. John's College opened its New Mexico campus on October 1, 1964. Situated on the east side of Santa Fe, the college adjoins the foothills of the Sangre de Cristo Mountains. Photo by Barry J. Drennon

During the late 1950s the college received so many applications for admission that the board of visitors and governors sought ways of providing a St. John's education to more students. Determined to maintain a small integrated community of scholars, school authorities quickly decided against enlarging the Annapolis facilities. When news of a possible expansion became public, the college received thirty-seven proposals from locations throughout the nation.

In January 1961 president Richard Weigle visited Santa Fe to consider an attractive offer of land made to St. John's by two prominent residents, Mr. and Mrs. John Gaw Meem. Recently retired, Meem had been one of New Mexico's leading architects. After Weigle's inspection, Santa Fe received a favorable report from a faculty committee that had toured the four most promising sites. The board of visitors and governors then voted to accept the Meems' offer and establish the second campus at its present location.

On October 1, 1964, the new institution opened its doors to its first class of eighty-four freshmen. Another class was added each year until the college had four full classes. Student population reached about 300 in 1981, and there it remains today.

As president of the college in the 1960s, Dr. Weigle supervised St. John's expansion into New Mexico. The bell tower was designed by John Gaw Meem, a Santa Fe architect who donated land for the campus. Photo by Barry J. Drennon

GREATER ALBUQUERQUE CHAMBER OF COMMERCE

Since its founding almost seventy years ago, the Greater Albuquerque Chamber of Commerce has actively supported the commercial and cultural development of the city's metropolitan area. On July 12, 1917, fifteen prominent businessmen met in the old Commercial Club at Fourth Street and Gold Avenue to establish a chamber of commerce after investigating similar groups in other towns. Although pleased with the growth that their community had enjoyed recently, the founders agreed that "cooperation and organization must be the order if Albuquerque is to maintain her stride." To stimulate enthusiasm and publicity, the organizers invited interested citizens to a gala banquet at the Masonic Temple. Following a program of oratory and musical selections, chamber leaders made plans for a city-wide membership drive that succeeded in enrolling 627 business men and women during a three-day campaign.

Soon after organizing, the chamber began its efforts to boost Albuquerque by distributing 15,000 promotional brochures that emphasized the region's salubrious climate. Health care, particularly the treatment of tuberculosis, had become a growth industry in the Southwest. Attracted by the high, dry environment, hundreds of invalids arrived each year seeking a cure in the desert sunshine. In 1918 Albuquerque, a town of 25,000, boasted nine hospitals and sanitariums, all competing for business with dozens of similar institutions from Texas to California. Fortunately, many patients regained their health and stayed in New Mexico to become valued members of the community.

On the eve of World War II the chamber realized an important long-range objective by securing a major air base for Albuquerque. After intensive lobbying by political and business leaders, military authorities established Kirtland Field, a training center for bomber crews, next to the city's commercial airport. Named for a pioneer Army aviator, Colonel Roy C. Kirtland, the installation soon expanded to include a school for aircraft mechanics known as Sandia Base. Today Kirtland ranks sixth among the nation's Air Force bases; its principal tenant is Sandia National Laboratories, Albuquerque's largest employer. A prime contractor for the Department of Energy, Sandia's main objective is the development of nuclear weapons and related space age technology.

Now located in Albuquerque's Convention Center, the Greater Albuquerque Chamber of Commerce has occupied four different offices since its founding in 1917. Shown is the North Fourth Street location. Expansion of the existing convention center has strong chamber support. Courtesy, Albuquerque Museum Photoarchives

In the 1980s the chamber will continue to address local issues. Education, bridges and other transportation issues, annexation issues, the Coors Corridor Study, small business, legislative issues, and issues affecting the quality of life are some of the items the chamber is addressing. The "Buy New Mexico" program is an ongoing project that encourages businesses to buy products from within the state whenever possible. Thanks to chamber support for projects such as these, Albuquerque has become one of the fastest-growing cities in the Southwest.

GAS COMPANY OF NEW MEXICO

One of the state's largest public utilities, the Gas Company of New Mexico is a division of Southern Union Company of Dallas. In 1929 legendary Texas oil man Clint Murchison organized Southern Union as a holding company that combined several southwestern gas distribution and pipeline businesses owned by the Murchison family and their associates. When incorporated, Southern Union's only New Mexico property was the city water franchise at Lovington, but the firm soon established other utilities and has become the state's leading natural gas distributor. Other interests include pipelines, oil and gas production, and a chain of stores retailing gas appliances. In 1976 Southern Union joined all of its New Mexico utility operations into one division, which was designated the Gas Company of New Mexico.

Soon after its organization, Southern Union executives realized that New Mexico offered a great potential demand for natural gas. Although the state already boasted some gas production, local distribution systems were virtually nonexistent. During a vacation in 1929, Murchison discovered that Albuquerque depended on manufactured gas from an antiquated plant built in 1890. Santa Fe had no gas service at all. Sensing an opportunity, Murchison and Wofford Cain went to the San Juan Basin in northwestern New Mexico where several gas wells had been drilled at Kutz Canyon near Bloomfield. After obtaining commitments from local producers, they secured a franchise to serve Farmington, then a sleepy agricultural town on the San Juan River. They also made plans to construct a pipeline over the Continental Divide to Santa Fe and Albuquerque. In October Southern Union formed a New Mexico subsidiary, predecessor to the present Gas Company.

Always enthusiastic, Murchison outbid two competitors for the Albuquerque franchise and agreed to post a $100,000 bond, far more cash than the organization had on hand. That seemed an enormous sum in the depths of the Depression but Southern Union's Dallas banker agreed to honor Murchison's check, thus assuring the project's success.

The energy crisis of the early 1970s provided strong incentives for exploration and drilling to supplement the nation's reserves of oil and gas.

Later, with the line almost completed, the business found itself strapped for cash. Fortunately, Albuquerque's colorful mayor, Clyde Tingley, approved a 50-percent reduction in the bond which allowed

Pipeline construction workers enjoyed few luxuries while building Southern Union's main gas line to Albuquerque in 1930.

Southern Union to meet its construction payroll. The firm arranged with Albuquerque Gas and Electric Company to provide retail distribution through its old manufactured gas system.

Despite many difficulties the line was completed. Service to Santa Fe began on October 21, 1930, with a ceremony in which Mayor James C. McConvery fired a roman candle into a tall standpipe. The resulting blaze lit up the countryside for miles while hundreds of Santa Feans cheered and honked their automobile horns. The company also began service to Clovis in the same year, using gas piped in from the Texas Panhandle. As its distribution lines spread, Southern Union initiated an aggressive campaign to demonstrate the advantages of gas over coal, wood, and kerosene. In Albuquerque eager salesmen sometimes loaned appliances to potential customers in their zeal to make converts.

The outbreak of World War II brought new challenges and opportunities to Southern Union. Despite shortages of pipe and other material, company personnel built and maintained gas systems for air bases at Carlsbad, Clovis, Roswell, and Albuquerque. When peace returned, many servicemen decided to stay in the Southwest, causing major population growth in Southern Union's trade area. Anticipating sales increases, the firm expanded its exploration activities to locate new reserves. Drilling proved particularly rewarding at the Barker Dome field in the San Juan Basin and diagonally across the state at the Empire and Red Lake fields in Eddy County. Between 1954 and 1960 Southern Union drilled 169 wells, resulting in 147 gas producers, 9 oil wells, and 13 dry holes.

Southern Union also enlarged its distribution network during the postwar years. Between 1949 and 1968 it provided service to many additional locations, including Alamogordo, Gallup, Silver City, and Roswell, through new franchises

During World War II women frequently replaced male Southern Union employees who had left the company to join the armed services to work in defense industries.

or merger with existing enterprises. After extended negotiations company executives purchased Albuquerque's retail system in 1949 during a meeting in Santa Fe's La Fonda Hotel with representatives from Public Service Company of New Mexico, successor to Albuquerque Gas and Electric. Increased use of natural gas to fuel irrigation pumps also brought new customers from agricultural areas on the state's east side. By 1956 Southern Union ranked twenty-fifth among the nation's gas utilities.

Despite its record of continued growth Southern Union recognized serious problems in its New Mexico operations as early as the 1950s. In 1959, and again ten years later, the firm sought rate increases from the state's Public Service Commission. Both requests received partial approval but only after long and costly appeals to the courts. Rapidly escalating gas prices during the energy crisis of the 1970s intensified the problem.

Because of the low return to its stockholders, Southern Union offered to sell its New Mexico gas utility operations. Its criterion for selling GCNM was selecting a new owner who would protect the divergent interests of stockholders, employees, and customers. The new proposed owner is Public Service Company of New Mexico. Negotiations are currently under way, and the transfer of ownership is expected to be completed in 1985.

Extensive work is ongoing in preparation for approval of the transfer of ownership with involved state and federal agencies. Meanwhile, Gas Company of New Mexico continues to serve over 84 percent of the state's customers including 300,000 residential, commercial, and industrial customers in eighty different communities. In 1983 some 1,200 employees received approximately twenty-five million dollars in wages and salaries. The Gas Company of New Mexico's president, James O. Carnes, also serves as senior vice-president of Southern Union.

Fruit farmers in the San Juan Valley sometimes use small gas burners in their orchards to prevent frost damage.

THE REGENT OF ALBUQUERQUE

One of Albuquerque's most prestigious hotels, the Regent, welcomed its first guests in September 1975 as the Albuquerque Inn. The hotel originated as an integral part of Albuquerque's "Metro Seventies" project, an ambitious proposal to curtail urban blight and rejuvenate the city's downtown. With support from business and political leaders, developers erected several high-rise buildings, providing new space for shops and offices. Clustered around a broad Civic Plaza, the new structures included First National Bank's First Plaza; Alvarado Square, built by Public Service Company of New Mexico; the Mountain Bell building; and the impressive Convention Center.

The Albuquerque Inn grew out of the cooperative efforts of planners and developers who recognized the need for a large, conveniently located establishment to complement the Convention Center. Designed by architect Ken Fuji of Fresno, California, the 300-room hotel is connected to the Convention Center and adjacent parking by underground corridors that offer easy access between the buildings.

In 1979 Regent International, a worldwide hotel chain, took over management of Albuquerque Inn and renamed it The Regent of Albuquerque. From headquarters in Hong Kong, Regent International operates a small number of luxury hotels that extend from New York to Bangkok. Founded by Robert H. Burns in 1971, the Regent Group emphasizes comfort and personal attention for guests in each of its member hotels.

After taking charge, the new proprietors began an extensive renovation to bring the Albuquerque property up to Regent standards. Directed by Ellen L. McCluskey Associates of New York, the changes have given the hotel's public areas and guest rooms a new feeling of lightness and intimacy. To reflect the regional ambience, the designers integrated several interesting examples of southwestern art into the decor. Although the remodeling was extensive, The Regent remained open through it all.

On October 29, 1982, The Regent greeted a particularly distinguished visitor, Great Britain's Prince Charles, who had come to New Mexico for the dedication of Armand Hammer World College of the American West. An international educational institution that promotes peace and understanding, the World College organization had recently acquired the buildings and grounds of the old Montezuma Hotel in Las Vegas, thanks to the generosity of Dr. Hammer. As president of the United World College International Council, the prince had joined Hammer and other dignitaries for opening ceremonics thc previous day.

To climax the royal tour and benefit the new school, World College supporters scheduled a formal reception and ball in Albuquerque's Convention Center. After greeting the prince, over 1,300 guests sat down to an elaborate dinner of chicken Montezuma and piñon mousse prepared by The Regent's chef. Since then, The Regent's dinner menu has continued to offer chicken Montezuma, the dish that was created originally for His Royal Highness, the Prince of Wales.

Famous for its cuisine, The Regent of Albuquerque has become the city's leading downtown hotel in the past five years.

NEW MEXICO FEDERAL SAVINGS AND LOAN ASSOCIATION

Most financial institutions originate in a large urban center and then expand into smaller neighboring communities, but New Mexico Federal Savings and Loan Association has successfully reversed that pattern. Organized at Taos in 1961, New Mexico Federal's predecessor, Northern Savings and Loan Association, opened for business in January 1963 in a small, poorly heated office near Kit Carson's old house.

The new organization immediately began soliciting savings accounts to supplement a meager $130,000 in subscribed capital. From that beginning, the association has developed into one of the state's largest thrift institutions with headquarters in Albuquerque and branches in Santa Fe, Española, and Taos.

Northern Savings and Loan was the brainchild of Stephen A. Mitchell, chairman of the Democratic National Committee from 1952 to 1955, the era when Adlai Stevenson dominated the party. A Chicago attorney, Mitchell also maintained a law practice in Taos and recognized a need for a savings and loan there.

Stephen A. Mitchell, co-founder of New Mexico Federal Savings and Loan Association, served as chairman of the Democratic National Committee in the early 1950s. In this publicity photo he posed with two donkeys, the party's traditional symbol.

In 1965 the firm changed its name to First Northern Savings and Loan Association and established itself in Santa Fe during the following year. Seeking new business, First Northern found a strong demand for mortgages and home improvement loans at Los Alamos when the Atomic Energy Commission began to sell off housing built for wartime projects to local residents. As growth in the north continued, the next step became obvious. To achieve its full potential, First Northern turned toward Albuquerque, the state's financial and population center.

As a young businessman Robert E. Morris joined Northern Savings and Loan, New Mexico Federal's predecessor at Taos in 1962. Today he serves as the association's president.

In 1975 First Northern purchased New Mexico Savings and Loan Association, a mortgage banking company with two Albuquerque offices. Joining the two associations offered many advantages but some knotty problems arose as well. Because NMSL was not a conventional savings and loan, the merger required almost two years of negotiations with government regulators to assure that accounts transferred to First Northern became covered by the federal depositors insurance program. In 1982 the firm adopted its present name, New Mexico Federal Savings and Loan Association.

Perhaps the greatest contribution made to the state's economy by New Mexico Federal and other savings and loans has been the attraction of capital to finance new development. Each time a mortgage is sold to federal agencies or other outside investors, the sales price returns to New Mexico for reinvestment. Recently thrift institutions have been put through a wringer caused by inflation, high interest rates, and ruthless competition from alternative savings programs. Despite present economic uncertainties the people at New Mexico Federal intend to provide necessary financial services to investors and borrowers as they have for the past twenty-two years.

W.C. KRUGER AND ASSOCIATES, ARCHITECTS & PLANNERS, INC.

Bataan Memorial Building, state capitol complex, Santa Fe, 1953.

Originating in a small office a block away from Santa Fe's famous plaza, W.C. Kruger and Associates has become one of the largest architectural firms in New Mexico. Since Willard C. Kruger first hung out his shingle over forty years ago, his organization has designed more than 500 projects for various clients in the public and private sectors. Now based in Albuquerque, the company maintains offices in Santa Fe and Las Cruces. Despite tremendous growth, Kruger and Associates has retained the philosophy that clients are best served through personal attention from teams of highly qualified specialists. Kruger personnel provide a wide variety of professional services including site selection, master planning, cost projections, and architectural design.

A native New Mexican, Willard Kruger was born in 1910 at Raton, where he attended local schools. Thanks to his athletic ability, Kruger received a basketball scholarship to Oklahoma State University, the nearest institution then offering a degree in architecture. After graduation in 1934 the young architect took a job with the New Mexico State Planning Board, but soon switched to the local office of the Federal Works Progress Administration. As head of the WPA's architectural department Kruger took on his first major project, design of Carrie Tingley Hospital for Crippled Children at Hot Springs (now Truth or Consequences).

Built by the WPA and operated by the state, Carrie Tingley Hospital was named for the wife of Clyde Tingley, who served two terms as New Mexico's governor during the New Deal era. Accompanied by Tingley, Kruger traveled to Warm Springs, Georgia, to study the famous hospital where President Franklin Delano Roosevelt had received treatment. After returning, he designed Carrie Tingley in Territorial architectural style, a local adaptation of Greek-revival style characterized by brick copings and pedimented doors and windows. Constructed with brick and tile manufactured at the state penitentiary, the 100-bed hospital admitted its first patients in September 1937. Its successful completion gave Kruger the impetus necessary to start his own architectural practice.

Following the outbreak of World War II Kruger became involved in an extremely important defense program, design of the original facilities for development of the atomic bomb at Los Alamos. In December 1942 he accompanied Dr. J. Robert Oppenheimer and Brigadier General Leslie R. Groves during an inspection tour of the future site of the Manhattan Project. Within days Kruger received his first government contract for building designs, street and utility layouts, and rehabilitation of Los Alamos Ranch School, which had been commandeered to serve as project headquarters. Working around the clock, construction crews had the first buildings ready for the scientists in mid-March.

During the past forty years the Kruger organization has continued to play an important role at Los Alamos. In addition to designing new technical facilities for the

Atomic Energy Commission and the Department of Energy, the firm also helped to change the town into a permanent community. Since 1946 the Kruger staff has drawn plans for residential subdivisions, schools, churches, and recreational sites. To improve and beautify the downtown, Kruger designed an innovative community center that won high praise from architectural critics.

In response to increasing demand for his services, Kruger organized W.C. Kruger and Associates in 1948. At that time the firm began implementation of a long-range development plan for several new buildings and rehabilitation of others in the state capitol complex in Santa Fe, all designed in Territorial style. The project began with construction of a new Land Office Building followed by a renovation of the state capitol in which the old pillared facade and domed roof were replaced by Territorial styling. Later it was renamed the Bataan Memorial Building in honor of those New Mexicans who fought at Bataan during World War II.

In the mid-1960s the state expansion program reached its climax with construction of a new capitol. The Kruger design superimposed Territorial styling on an all-round facade reminiscent of a Pueblo Indian kiva. Known as "the Round House" since its completion in 1966, the new statehouse aroused a storm of controversy among New Mexicans because of its unconventional appearance.

With the new capitol completed, the Kruger organization became increasingly active, producing work in such volume in the past twenty years that only a few examples can be mentioned here. At the University of New Mexico the firm designed several buildings including Woodward Lecture Hall, the Humanities Building, and the recently completed Biomedical Research Facility for the School of Medicine. In the technical field Kruger personnel designed highly specialized installations at Kirtland Air Force Base, White Sands Proving Grounds, Sandia Base, and Los Alamos National Laboratory. The staff has also produced plans for many banks, churches, hospitals, schools, hotels, and office buildings located throughout the Southwest.

In the 1950s the Kruger organization recruited two of its present executives, Marion C. Smith and J.W. Keeran. Smith came to New Mexico after having graduated from Texas A&M and obtaining his registration in Texas. The company's primary project architect, he became its president in 1984. Keeran is a certified public accountant who now serves as the firm's secretary/treasurer. An expert in financial management, he has been in charge of contract negotiations and fee arrangements with clients.

On June 5, 1984, Willard C. Kruger died, thus ending his fifty-year career as architect and planner. His co-workers have been shaken by their loss but continuity at Kruger and Associates is assured under the leadership of Marion Smith and J.W. Keeran.

Humanities Building, University of New Mexico, Albuquerque, 1974.

Albuquerque Bank of Commerce, now renamed United New Mexico, Albuquerque.

VALLIANT COMPANY

In this 1941 photo George P. Valliant (center), who now serves as chief executive officer, is flanked by his father George S. (left) and Arthur A. Allen, one of the firm's founders.

Hoping to find greater opportunity in the Southwest, the Valliant family sold the daily newspaper that they had published in Texarkana, Arkansas, and moved to Albuquerque in 1914. After arriving in New Mexico, George E. Valliant, his son, George S. Valliant, and their business partner, Arthur A. Allen, bought the *Albuquerque Evening Herald,* an afternoon paper that favored the Republican party. As staunch Democrats, the three partners soon changed the *Herald's* political affiliation, making it a champion of Democratic principles.

After five years in the newspaper business, the two Valliants and Allen sold the *Herald* in 1919 to two experienced journalists, Thomas Hughes and H.B. Hening. Turning to a new venture, the partners bought Albright and Anderson Printing Co., a firm that specialized in business cards, letterheads, and office forms. The company also produced all kinds of publications and advertising brochures in both color and black and white. In 1922 Albright and Anderson became the Valliant Company.

Once established in Albuquerque, George S. Valliant soon became a wheelhorse in Democratic politics. During the New Deal era he was able to make good use of his political connections as the Democrats became the dominant party in the state. In the 1930s and 1940s the Valliant Company received a number of contracts for the printing of *New Mexico Magazine* and other material produced by the state's tourist bureau. At election time the firm also printed large quantities of ballots and other forms used at the polls.

In 1937 George S. Valliant's only son, George P., graduated from Virginia Military Institute and came back to Albuquerque to work in the family print shop. Recalled to military duty following Pearl Harbor, the younger Valliant served for four years as a cavalry officer in Texas, the Philippines, and Japan. After his discharge in 1945, George P. Valliant returned to the Valliant Company and began working his way up through the managerial ranks.

Five years later George S. Valliant died, leaving his son in charge of an enterprise that soon faced serious problems. During a wave of reform in the early 1950s, New Mexico's legislature passed a State Purchasing Act requiring that all state contracts for goods and services be subject to competitive bidding. Since rivals could easily undercut previous bids by small amounts, the new legislation made it increasingly difficult for the Valliants to retain state printing contracts.

To take up the slack George P. Valliant expanded his business and diversified into new product lines. Through acquisitions, the Valliant Company established itself in the office supply and office furniture fields and began production of carbon business forms for the first time. The strategy has proved successful and has made Valliant foremost in its field in the Albuquerque area. Two sons, Dennis P. and George K., have joined George P. Valliant in company management.

Located at 611-615 Gold Avenue Southwest in downtown Albuquerque, the Valliant Company's printing plant was built in 1941.

TINNIN ENTERPRISES

Robert P. Tinnin, Sr. (left), and son Thomas P. Tinnin, chairman of the board and president, respectively, of Tinnin Enterprises.

Although Tinnin Enterprises is a growing company, its board chairman, Robert P. Tinnin, Sr., has been prominent in Albuquerque's business community for over fifty years. In 1981 Tinnin and other family members merged their interests in various family corporations into what is now known as Tinnin Enterprises. His son, Thomas P. Tinnin, is currently president of Tinnin Enterprises and is a general agent for Transamerica Occidental Life Insurance Company. His brother, Bob, who is a partner and attorney with one of Albuquerque's prominent law firms, was president of the State Bar Association in 1984. He too has been instrumental in the success and growth of the family business as an active participant and investor.

Born at Hornersville, Missouri, a small town on the Arkansas border, Bob Tinnin came to New Mexico as a boy in 1916. Eager for an education, he attended Montezuma College at Las Vegas and then transferred to Tyler College at Tyler, Texas, where he studied business administration and cotton purchasing and grading. After graduating from Tyler, Tinnin went to work as a cotton buyer at Artesia in eastern New Mexico for George H. McFadden and Brothers, Dallas brokers.

Unfortunately, the cotton trade offered few opportunities in the late 1920s, forcing Bob Tinnin to seek other employment. In the depths of the Depression he secured a position in Phoenix, Arizona, selling corporate and municipal bonds for National Guarantee Syndicate, a Phoenix investment house. Later Tinnin switched to the insurance business, in which he established a successful career. In 1943 he became general agent for Occidental Life Insurance Company of California. Tinnin subsequently became interested in real estate, initiating several important ventures such as Highland Shopping Center and Tinnin Shopping Center in Albuquerque's Southeast and Northeast Heights, respectively.

When he entered the business world, Tom Tinnin followed a path similar to his father's. In 1969 he left the University of New Mexico for two years in Washington as an aide to Clinton P. Anderson, then a United States senator. Homesick for the Southwest, Tom returned to Albuquerque and entered the insurance business after graduating from the university in 1973. Within ten years he had become a member of the Million Dollar Round Table, the life insurance industry's prestigious sales society.

With his insurance agency going well, Tom Tinnin began to make some profitable investments in real estate. His investments have been profitable not only for himself but have been beneficial to the family real estate interests as well. These investments cover a wide range of areas, from farming and shopping centers to apartments and town houses. His success has attracted national attention, notably a feature story in the March 1984 edition of *Money* magazine.

Throughout his career Tom Tinnin has received enthusiastic encouragement from his father. Thus, the organization of Tinnin Enterprises in 1981 seemed the natural culmination of years of mutual admiration and respect. Tom sees a bright and growing future for Tinnin Enterprises.

ELLIOTT ENTERPRISES, INC.
La Placita Dining Rooms

Indians display their goods for sale outside the famous La Placita Dining Rooms in Old Albuquerque.

La Placita's historic walnut staircase, complemented today by regional art, leads to the La Placita Art Gallery and office.

A family corporation, Elliott Enterprises owns and operates La Placita, one of Albuquerque's most popular restaurants. Situated in a rambling adobe building in the historic Old Town neighborhood, La Placita is famous for southwestern atmosphere and authentic New Mexican cuisine. Company president Dale Elliott is quick to point out that only traditional ingredients go into the array of tantalizing dishes prepared in his kitchen. Dale and his father, Elmer Elliott, acquired the business over thirty years ago at the urging of Dale's mother, who not only loved Mexican food but also recognized the restaurant's economic potential.

A Texas hotel man, Elmer Elliott became the owner of New Mexico's largest restaurant when he bought the Court Cafe in downtown Albuquerque during World War II. After his discharge from the U.S. Army Air Force in 1945, Dale Elliott became his father's partner. To improve his managerial skills, Dale enrolled for two years of study in the hotel and restaurant school at Cornell University.

On evenings away from the Court, the family frequently enjoyed dining at a small Mexican restaurant in Old Town. When an opportunity arose, the Elliotts bought the business in 1953 and opened La Placita after extensive renovation. Presently the restaurant seats 275 people in five dining rooms and retains fifty to seventy employees. Dale's son Rick and his wife, Virginia, purchased the firm upon Dale's retirement on November 1, 1984. A granddaughter also works as a busgirl, representing the fourth generation employed at La Placita.

In 1980 La Placita became entangled in a landmark lawsuit when the Elliotts sought to obtain a license allowing sale of alcoholic beverages to diners. Because the restaurant is located within 300 feet of San Felipe de Neri Church, state law required a waiver from Albuquerque's City Council prior to license approval. The waiver request aroused immediate objections from a group of San Felipe parishioners who believed that Old Town was becoming over-commercialized and was in danger of deteriorating into something akin to Bourbon Street in New Orleans.

On July 28 the council granted the waiver but opponents appealed to the courts on grounds that city officials had violated the state's "open meeting" law by failing to provide a room large enough to accommodate all those who wished to attend the hearing. Eventually New Mexico's Supreme Court ruled that the meeting had been valid. Meanwhile, during its 1981 session, the state legislature authorized issuance of beer and wine licenses to eating establishments despite heavy lobbying by liquor interests. Seizing that option, the Elliotts dropped plans to secure a full-service license and applied for one of the new permits instead. The change failed to mollify the opposition but, after further costly litigation, La Placita finally received authorization to sell beer and wine with meals, thus resolving the issue.

The famous "Tree Room" at the La Placita Dining Rooms.

HOOTEN/STAHL INC. REALTORS

In March 1967 two young executives, Bill Hooten and Jack Stahl, resigned their positions with an Albuquerque lending institution and organized Hooten/Stahl Realtors. Eager to start their own business, the partners had gained some experience by investing in apartment buildings and other small developments. Determined to keep their operation small, with a minimum of outside help, Hooten and Stahl set up shop in a tiny, two-room office at 1313 San Pedro Drive Northeast. Business was good from the start, however, forcing them to move into larger quarters and hire office personnel and salesmen. Within three years Hooten/Stahl had become Albuquerque's leading real estate firm, a position it has retained ever since.

In many ways Hooten and Stahl had remarkably similar backgrounds. Born in Arkansas, Bill Hooten grew up in Las Cruces, New Mexico, but, after completing his education, he returned to his native state to coach football at North Little Rock High School. Hooten later returned to New Mexico and entered the real estate business at Roswell. In 1962 he joined the Roswell office of New Mexico Savings and Loan Association and was transferred to Albuquerque the following year. Jack Stahl moved to Albuquerque from Illinois because of a severe asthmatic condition. A graduate of the University of New Mexico, he taught at Albuquerque's Ernie Pyle Junior High School and then set up a real estate venture known as Housefinders. With some persuasion from Hooten, Stahl joined the staff of New Mexico Savings and Loan in 1965.

Once established, Hooten/Stahl handled all kinds of real estate transactions including commercial properties, vacant land, and residential housing. Subsequently the firm became active in leasing, property management, and subdividing. From the beginning Hooten/Stahl sought to increase profits by adopting new business methods.

Bill Hooten at the premier showing of Towne Park, April 1984.

In 1977 Jack Stahl left the firm to start a new real estate business of his own. Bill Hooten bought his partner's equity but retained the old name. Under his leadership Hooten/Stahl has pursued a wide range of interests and continues to be one of the most innovative and dynamic real estate companies in Albuquerque.

Assuming responsibility for sales, Hooten/Stahl managed the conversion of the 292-unit Winrock Apartments to condominiums, the first changeover of its kind in Albuquerque. The subdivision of Towne Park has proved to be another successful Hooten/Stahl innovation. Comprised of houses in the $60-80,000 range, Towne Park is located on land owned by the University of New Mexico south of the intersection of Eubank Boulevard and Interstate Highway 40. Enhanced by an attractive clubhouse, sauna baths, and jogging paths, the development has provided reasonably priced housing for its residents and additional income for the university. Pleased with the results, the State Land Office is considering similar developments on other tracts under its jurisdiction.

BLAKE'S LOTABURGER, INC.

The first Lotaburger store opened at San Mateo and Southern in Albuquerque on July 9, 1952. Today the chain encompasses sixty-six facilities in New Mexico and three in Phoenix, Arizona.

Like many newly returned veterans in the 1950s, Blake Chanslor had no interest in going back to his old job at a Texas Panhandle oil refinery. Determined to make a new life for himself, he moved his family to Albuquerque after his discharge from the U.S. Navy. In July 1952 Chanslor and his wife, June, scraped together $5,300, which they invested in a small hamburger stand at the corner of San Mateo and Southern in southeast Albuquerque. Before leaving Texas he had gained some experience in a similar business owned by relatives at Pampa.

Known as Lotaburger, Chanslor's first stand sold only hamburgers and potato chips. Thirsty customers obtained soft drinks from two coin-operated machines beside the tiny, 270-square-foot building. Because help was hard to get, Blake and June spent many long hours at the grill frying burgers. San Mateo had been paved only recently, and the neighborhood boasted few other businesses at the time. The stand quickly attracted a loyal clientele, however, thanks largely to heavy traffic from nearby Kirtland Air Force Base and Sandia Laboratories.

In January 1953 the Chanslors opened a second Lotaburger a few miles north on San Mateo at the corner of Menaul Boulevard, the beginning of the firm's phenomenal expansion. By the end of that year the owners had established three more outlets, including one at Santa Fe, their first out-of-town branch. Since that time the Lotaburger chain has grown to sixty-six stores in New Mexico and three in Phoenix, Arizona. The company headquarters remains at Albuquerque in a large two-story building that houses business offices, a warehouse for produce, condiments, and other supplies, and facilities for processing the thousands of hamburger patties consumed daily.

Although the menu has broadened considerably, the basic operation remains much the same as in the original store. Accounts receivable are never a problem since all business is done for cash. Despite the intrusion of nationally franchised competition, advertising costs are minimal because the product sells itself with assistance from a host of satisfied customers.

In recent years Lotaburger has established a real estate subsidiary, Celco Investments, Inc., to handle acquisition of new locations. The firm also operates its own carpentry and sheet-metal shops to build and maintain its many outlets. Refrigeration experts are also always on call at the central office to repair cooling systems at any Lotaburger store.

Although Lotaburger has developed into a large corporation during the past thirty years, it has continued to be a family business. Blake Chanslor is still president and chief executive officer. June Chanslor's assistance is no longer required at the grill but she keeps her hand in by serving as the firm's secretary/treasurer. Two sons are also active in management.

The firm's headquarters and commissary in Albuquerque.

UNITED NEW MEXICO

Oldest among United New Mexico's family of banks, the venerable First National Bank of Roswell was founded in 1890. This impressive structure at the corner of Third and Main streets served as the bank's main office from 1894 to 1912.

A young and vigorous bank holding company, United New Mexico Financial Corporation has deep roots in the state, particularly in the south and east. Organized in 1967 as Bank Securities, Inc., United New Mexico includes some of the oldest financial institutions in New Mexico. The firm's history began in 1912, when R.D. Champion, a Tularosa merchant, obtained a one-third interest in the brand-new First State Bank of Tularosa for $5,000. Five years later he was president. Seeking greater opportunity, Champion moved the bank's main offices thirteen miles south to Alamogordo in 1933. Later he changed its name to Security Bank and Trust Company. Just before his death in 1957 Champion turned over the presidency of Security Bank to his grandson, Ted Bonnell, who had joined the staff at Alamogordo seven years earlier.

While serving as Security's chief executive in the 1960s, Bonnell realized that New Mexico's dynamic economy required larger concentrations of capital to achieve optimum growth. Recognizing the potential for a well-financed bank holding company, Bonnell joined a group of businessmen, including his brothers, Kenneth and Dorsey, to form Bank Securities, Inc., in 1967. Envisioned as a network of locally directed banks under common ownership, BSI started operations by acquiring First State Bank of Cuba in 1968 and installing Kenneth Bonnell as president. The holding company added American Bank of Carlsbad to its chain later that same year.

BSI began successfully but, in order to establish itself as a major lender, it needed an affiliate in Albuquerque, the state's largest city and financial hub. To enter that market, BSI brought American Bank of Commerce into the system in 1970. Shortly thereafter American Bank moved into new headquarters, a thirteen-story high rise at the corner of Lomas Boulevard and Second Street that now also houses the main offices of United New Mexico. Successfully established in Albuquerque, BSI continued to grow in other areas. By 1973 the corporation owned or controlled additional banks in Roswell, Portales, Vaughn, Ruidoso, and Rio Rancho.

After spreading over much of New Mexico, BSI underwent a change of ownership in 1979. Robert O. Anderson, a prominent oil man and financier from Roswell, his two sons, Robert B. and Phelps Anderson, and A.G. Hamilton of Carlsbad took control by purchasing 200,000 shares of BSI stock for ten million dollars. With new leadership in charge, BSI acquired banks at Deming and Socorro and opened a new bank in Santa Fe. On March 1, 1984, Bank Securities, Inc., became United New Mexico Financial Corporation. Local affiliates have adopted the name United New Mexico with the appropriate geographical location added. United New Mexico now controls eleven banks with forty-two branches and is well positioned to provide a full range of financial services to customers throughout the state.

In September 1973 American Bank of Commerce moved into its new thirteen-story office facility at Second and Lomas. The building, which was the first in the Albuquerque Urban Renewal Project, is also the headquarters of United New Mexico Financial Corporation.

ATKINSON TRADING COMPANY

While operating Three Hogans, the Atkinson family made their home in a Navajo hogan. A young Nancy Atkinson poses for this photo, taken about 1940.

According to Joe Atkinson, president of Atkinson Trading Company, Indian trading has been in his family's blood for generations. When the firm was incorporated at Gallup in 1972, the family already had almost sixty years' experience in the business. As traders, the Atkinsons have seen some hard times but, through hard work and perseverance, they have made their enterprise into one of the nation's largest dealers in Indian arts and crafts. From headquarters in Albuquerque, Atkinson Trading Company now operates a popular restaurant in Old Town, sales outlets in New Mexico and Arizona, and a large facility in Gallup for its handmade jewelry production.

The family first came to New Mexico in 1914, when Joe Atkinson's great-uncle, Tobe Turpen, left his home in Alvarado, Texas, and headed west, eventually settling at Gallup on the edge of the vast Navajo reservation. Once established as a dealer in livestock and Indian curios, Turpen encouraged his sister, Sue, and her husband, Willard Bollin, to come out from Texas to help in the business. In 1934 the Bollins' daughter, Wilmerine, also moved to New Mexico accompanied by her high school sweetheart, Leroy Atkinson. Soon after their arrival the young couple were married. During their years at Gallup the Atkinsons raised five children—a daughter and four sons, including their adopted Navajo son, "Little" Leroy.

Faced with new responsibilities, Atkinson went to work for Jack Hill, a Gallup merchant specializing in the Navajo trade. Hill maintained a general store where his Indian customers purchased all kinds of goods including coffee, sugar, dry goods, hardware, cooking utensils, saddles, and harness, usually on credit. In return he received large quantities of wool, mohair, sheep, and piñon nuts. He also took in Navajo rugs and jewelry through pawn or outright purchase. As an apprentice, Atkinson quickly learned the value of Indian products and the proper etiquette for dealing with Navajos. Within a few years he was put in charge of the Three Hogans trading post just west of the Arizona border on U.S. Highway 66.

Determined to have a business of his own, Leroy Atkinson left Hill in 1943 and built a new trading post at Box Canyon twenty miles west of Gallup. Unlike Three Hogans, which was patronized mainly by Indians, Box Canyon appealed to the growing number of motorists driving along Route 66. In those days highway storekeepers depended on the hard sell to draw in tourists, using outrageous gimmicks like snake farms as promotions. Not to be outdone, Atkinson erected a pair of enormous cavemen as enticements for travelers. Despite the campy

Leroy and Wilmerine Atkinson flank employee A.L. "Two-Gun" Bailey. The Navajo boy in the foreground later became an expert silversmith. Photo circa 1940

advertising, the merchandise at Box Canyon included top-quality craftsmanship. To assure an adequate supply of authentic Indian jewelry, Atkinson supplied silver and turquoise to Navajo smiths who turned out rings, bracelets, and necklaces for sale at the trading post. This procedure has proven so successful that it is still practiced by the Atkinson Trading Company today. After ten years beside the highway the Atkinsons moved from Box Canyon to Tucson, where they opened a shop dealing exclusively in Indian arts and crafts.

In 1962 the Atkinsons' son Joe returned to Gallup following his discharge from the U.S. Navy. Hoping to continue in the family tradition, he set himself up as an Indian trader. With $175 in his pocket, Joe Atkinson paid out $125 to rent a store building north of the railroad tracks where he established the Covered Wagon trading post. His remaining fifty dollars was invested in a showcase. To finance his initial inventory, Joe sold part of the goods on hand for cash and then raced to the bank to cover the check he had given as a down payment. When the balance came due several months later, he had accumulated enough profits to pay off the debt.

The store soon became popular with the Navajos, who came in to buy groceries and other merchandise in exchange for the usual jewelry, sheep, wool, and pelts. With the proceeds Joe opened a tourist-oriented trading post in downtown Gallup and his father came in as manager. In 1972 the family organized the present Atkinson Trading Company. To take advantage of the Indian jewelry craze that swept the nation in the early 1970s, the firm built a larger facility in Gallup employing over 100 Navajo silversmiths.

With jewelry production assured, the Atkinsons moved aggressively into retail sales in 1977 through purchase of eleven stores from Gilbert Ortega, a leading dealer in Indian artifacts. Extending from Dallas to Scottsdale, the chain did a big business but not all the outlets proved profitable, particularly after enthusiasm for Indian crafts began to fade in the late 1970s. Recently most of the stores have been sold. Those retained include one at Cameron, Arizona, midway between Flagstaff and the Grand Canyon, and another twenty miles west of Albuquerque where Interstate 40 crosses the Rio Puerco.

In 1981 Atkinson Trading Company purchased La Hacienda, a well-known restaurant on Albuquerque's Old Town plaza. The building originated as a handsome turn-of-the-century brick mansion but it was later remodeled in Spanish-pueblo style. Following a renovation the Atkinsons established company headquarters upstairs. On the ground floor, part of the restaurant has been converted into a sales outlet for the firm's stock in trade, Indian artifacts.

Leroy and Wilmerine Atkinson are proud of the fact that all of their children and grandchildren have continued in the business. With four generations of history in Indian trading, the Atkinsons can look with pride on the past and ahead to a bright future.

Located twenty miles west of Gallup on U.S. Highway 66, Box Canyon Trading Post attracted thousands of tourists traveling by car and bus.

KOOGLE AND POULS ENGINEERING, INC.

The original office of Koogle and Pouls was located in this building in Albuquerque.

In many ways Koogle and Pouls Engineering, Inc., conforms to the popular stereotype of a rapidly growing, high-technology company based in the Sun Belt. Organized at Albuquerque in 1964 by Herbert G. Koogle and Basil G. Pouls, the firm provides specialized services in the fields of civil engineering and land surveying. During their years together, the two founders have seen the surveyor's transit and chain almost entirely replaced by space age equipment undreamed of a short time ago. New techniques have been developed such as photogrammetrics, a complex process for producing maps and surveys from aerial photographs. Through imaginative use of advanced technology, Koogle and Pouls Engineering has established a leadership position within the profession and maintained an enviable record of growth.

Before starting their own business, Koogle and Pouls worked together for several years at F.M. Limbaugh Co., an Albuquerque engineer and land surveyor. A graduate of Stanford University, Koogle had previous experience with construction contractors on large building projects and in the design of water, sewage, and highway facilities. He now serves as president and chief engineer of Koogle and Pouls. Executive vice-president Basil Pouls has a degree in civil engineering from Massachusetts Institute of Technology. As a previous projects administrator and coordinator he brought extensive professional expertise to the firm. In 1972 the company's third officer and director, vice-president J. Robert Martinez, joined Koogle and Pouls Engineering. A former employee of the New Mexico State Highway Department, Martinez was an experienced surveyor and designer.

To improve their services to clients, company personnel are always searching for technological innovations within their profession. This is particularly true of photogrammetrics, which has developed into one of the most important divisions at Koogle and Pouls. Aerial photographs are obtained from a turbocharged Cessna 206 aircraft that has been specially modified to increase control and maneuverability. The highly sophisticated camera equipment on board is capable of rendering precise measurements from small fractions of an inch to many miles in length. Data derived from the photographs is extremely useful in locating highways, utility lines, subdivisions, and other projects. Archaeologists and mine operators find photogrammetry invaluable as a means of recording site information as it exists at a particular moment.

During the past few years Koogle and Pouls Engineering has made increasing use of computers for interactive graphics and to store and retrieve information provided by aerial photographs. Survey and engineering calculations are routinely run through the computer system, which also has the capacity to make contour maps and perform many graphic functions. Such equipment is expensive but the results are cost-effective and make Koogle and Pouls Engineering, Inc., competitive in this swiftly changing technological age.

The firm's current headquarters is on Comanche Northeast in Albuquerque.

SPERRY CORPORATION

Two years before New Mexico became a state, the company that was to become its largest industrial employer in the 1980s was born in New York. Founded in 1910, the Sperry Gyroscope Company has grown into Sperry Corporation, a world leader in high-technology electronic systems.

In 1980 Sperry's Aerospace & Marine Group Defense Systems Division established headquarters in Albuquerque. Aerospace & Marine Group is the company unit that can most directly trace its ancestry to the aeronautical pioneering tradition of the Sperry family.

It was Elmer Sperry who first recognized the potential of the gyroscope for aircraft stabilization. And it was the innovative genius of Elmer, his sons, and their first employees that created the first aircraft "autopilot," and flight instruments that made possible Jimmy Doolittle's first "blind" flight and the first successful solo flight around the world by Wiley Post.

Flight equipment and the premier company developing it have come a long way in the seven decades since Sperry was formed. Sophisticated television-type displays have replaced mechanical artificial horizons in a pilot's panel. And airborne microprocessors have advanced aviation from seat-of-the-pants daredevilry to precise science.

But in spite of a generation of advancement, the innovative spirit of the Sperrys is alive today in the company that bears their name.

Today in Albuquerque, a new generation of aerospace pioneers is contributing to America's security by conceiving, designing, and building systems to improve the capabilities of the country's airborne defense forces. Sperry's products for defense aircraft include automatic flight-control systems, electronic displays, multiplex data devices, reference systems, and aerial targets.

These systems are the quality standard on virtually every type of Free World military aircraft. Sperry's New Mexico employees are working to enhance the performance of such new aircraft as the Air Force B-lB strategic bomber, the AH-64 and Advanced Scout Army helicopters, and fighter aircraft for the Air Force, Navy, Marines, and NATO.

In addition, Sperry technology is helping extend the useful life of older military aircraft including the B-52, currently undergoing an avionics update, and the vintage F-100 fighter, being converted by Sperry into a remotely piloted target drone.

Sperry began operations in Albuquerque in summer 1980 at a leased facility at 2421 Aztec. The company opened its headquarters facility at 9201 San Mateo Boulevard Northeast in August 1981.

An expansion of the facility, completed in early 1983, brought the size of Sperry's plant to 290,000 square feet. An additional 208,000 square feet is due for completion by the fall of 1985.

With its commitment to innovation and excellence, Sperry Corporation will continue to contribute to America's defense, Albuquerque's economic growth and stability, and its employees' well-being for many years to come. With pride in its history, Sperry looks to the future.

Sperry Corporation's original Albuquerque Defense Systems Division plant opened its doors in 1980; it has undergone two expansions since then.

The world's first autopilot, shown here, was developed by Elmer Sperry. The autopilot's descendant, the Flight Control System, remains a major Sperry product line today in Albuquerque.

PUBLIC SERVICE COMPANY OF NEW MEXICO

In addition to housing the offices of Public Service Company of New Mexico, Alvarado Square also contains an interesting assortment of shops and restaurants.

During the 1880s venturesome businessmen brought electrical service to New Mexico's larger towns and cities for the first time. Citizens marveled at the technological miracle but, frequently, undercapitalization prevented those pioneer utility businesses from becoming profitable. As in many western states, economic realities forced consolidation with larger corporations backed by eastern capital. In New Mexico, a New York holding company, Federal Light and Power, dominated the industry after acquiring electric companies in Albuquerque, Santa Fe, Las Vegas, Belen, and Deming.

With the infusion of capital from Federal, the local companies grew and flourished. To improve service, the corporation constructed new generating plants at Deming and Las Vegas. The firm also erected a 44,000-volt transmission line, the first of its kind in the state, between Albuquerque and Santa Fe. In the 1930s Federal's subsidiary, Albuquerque Gas and Electric Company, obtained a reliable fuel source for expanded power production when Southern Union Company built a natural gas pipeline into the city from northwestern New Mexico.

The state's utilities came of age under Federal management, but during the New Deal era all such holding companies experienced increasing scrutiny from Washington. In 1935 Congress passed the Wheeler-Rayburn Act, intended to eliminate monopolistic abuses by the industry. The law contained a "death sentence" clause that ordered dissolution of utility holding companies within five years. As a result, Federal changed into a local corporation through salc of all its properties except those in New Mexico. With approval from various regulatory agencies, Federal in 1946 merged its affiliates across the state in Public Service Company of New Mexico. The older company was dissolved after stockholders received shares in PNM. In 1969 PNM received approval for listing on the New York Stock Exchange, ensuring a national market for its securities.

PNM's reorganization occurred at a fortuitous time. Between 1950 and 1960 Albuquerque's population more than doubled from 95,000 to 202,000, and other urban areas within the state experienced substantial increases. Company officials soon realized rapid growth would require additional generation and transmission facilities. To meet anticipated demand, PNM built two oil- and gas-fired plants near Albuquerque and established a new transmission grid connecting Albuquerque, Santa Fe, Las Vegas, and Belen.

Looking further into the future,

The PNM of yesteryear, Albuquerque Gas and Electric maintained headquarters at the southeast corner of Fifth and Central in 1928.

Before the advent of automobiles, this determined-looking repair crew and canine companion posed beside their horse-drawn vehicle.

PNM began acquiring leases in northwestern New Mexico's rich coal fields, anticipating reduced supplies and higher costs for natural gas. As gas prices rose in the 1960s, the company joined with five other utilities to erect the coal-fired Four Corners Generating Station near Farmington in which PNM owns a 13-percent interest. During the same decade the company laid plans for construction of San Juan Generating Station, another coal-fired installation also located in the Four Corners region. When the plant's fourth and final unit began operations in April 1982, San Juan enabled PNM's generating capacity to be almost 100-percent coal fired. The plant's equipment includes some of the world's most sophisticated pollution-control devices.

To secure further flexibility and lessen dependence on any single fuel source, PNM in the 1970s committed to a 10.3-percent participation in the projected Palo Verde Nuclear Generating Station being constructed in Arizona. When Palo Verde is completed in the mid-1980s, the plant will provide an alternate fuel source and ensure adequate energy supplies for future growth.

In addition to producing and distributing electricity, PNM also holds a municipal water franchise at Santa Fe under long-term contract. Early in 1985 the firm acquired the Gas Company of New Mexico as part of an overall settlement of a five-year-old, $122-million class action lawsuit against Southern Union Company of Dallas and four natural gas producers. Plaintiffs, including PNM, a residential gas consumer class, and certain state agencies, charged the defendants had conspired to fix natural gas prices in New Mexico, resulting in overcharges to consumers. The acquisition received approvals from certain state and federal regulatory agencies. PNM began operating the gas utility on January 28, 1985, with a program to renegotiate gas supply contracts in hope of lowering natural gas costs to New Mexico customers.

PNM established a diversification strategy to broaden its earning base and potential while contributing to the economic development of New Mexico. Two wholly owned subsidiaries were formed: Sunbelt Mining Company, Inc., and Meadows Resources, Inc. Sunbelt acquires, develops, and markets coal and other mineral resources, and provides related contract mining services for PNM and other regional customers. Meadows Resources, Inc., is the investment arm of PNM.

Meadows has three major business areas: Montaña de Fibra, Bellamah Community Development, and a venture capital portfolio. Montaña de Fibra, a medium-density fiberboard plant, was formed with Ponderosa Products, Inc. Fiberboard is a solid wood substitute used in the fabrication of quality furniture, cabinets, and related products. Meadows is also an equal partner in the land-development business with Bellamah Associates Ltd. Known as Bellamah Community Development, the joint venture purchases tracts of land near major southwestern cities and develops lots for sale to residential, commercial, and industrial builders. The firm, headquartered in Albuquerque, has regional offices in New Mexico, Arizona, Colorado, Texas, and Oklahoma. The venture capital portfolio includes investments in Pulse Systems, Inc., a New Mexico company that produces pulsed gas lasers for research and industrial use, and Zwan Magnetics, Inc., which uses thin-film technology to produce rigid disks for the computer industry.

Utility companies formerly displayed appliances in their office buildings to boost energy consumption. This 1931 photo shows the latest models in electric ranges and other appliances.

HONEYWELL, INC.

One of many high-technology companies moving into New Mexico, Honeywell, Inc., recently established a large micro-electronics plant in Albuquerque. Situated on the city's booming west side, the 100,000-square-foot plant manufactures sophisticated devices for environmental control and energy conservation. Although the company is new to New Mexico, Honeywell will celebrate its l00th anniversary in 1985. The firm was organized in Minneapolis as the Butz Thermo Electric Regulator Company by Albert M. Butz, an inventor who pioneered automatic temperature control. By connecting a thermostat with a spring motor, Butz developed a device that regulated furnace dampers according to temperature changes. Renamed the Minneapolis Heat Regulator Company in 1912, Butz' business became Minneapolis-Honeywell fifteen years later through a merger with Honeywell Heating Specialties Company of Wabash, Indiana. In 1964 the name was shortened to Honeywell, Inc.

Before selecting the Albuquerque site, Honeywell executives conducted an extensive survey of possible alternatives. They quickly agreed, however, that New Mexico's largest city met every qualification. Besides a Sun Belt location, Albuquerque offered a work force with an appropriate mix of skills for electronic manufacturing. Preliminary study showed a favorable state tax structure and reasonable wage levels. Once a decision had been reached, the company acquired a twenty-acre site on the West Mesa and began construction.

Completed in 1980, the Albuquerque plant produces thermostats and other environmental-control systems for houses and light commercial buildings such as restaurants or supermarkets. The facility is part of Honeywell's Residential Division, which operates other factories in the Minneapolis area; Gardena, California; and Chihuahua, Mexico. Residential Division is part of Control Products, one of five basic business units of Honeywell. Other basic business units include Aerospace and Defense, Control Systems, International Systems, and Information Systems.

Another division of Control Products, Micro Switch, opened a new facility in Las Cruces in 1982. Micro Switch designs and produces keyboard membrane assemblies and membrane touch panels. These products, used worldwide, are found in computer terminals, office equipment, consumer appliances, and machine tools.

While establishing itself in New Mexico, Honeywell quickly became attuned to community needs. In November 1983 company management joined with colleagues across town at Sandia National Laboratories to sponsor a conference of the American Indian Science and Engineering Society. Attended by about 300 college and high school students from throughout the country, the meeting was intended to encourage native Americans to seek careers as scientists and engineers. Speakers included Petson Zah, chairman of the Navajo tribe; Gilbert Peña, vice-chairman of the All-Indian Pueblo Council; Gerald Dinneen, Honeywell vice-president of corporate science and technology; and George Dacy, Sandia's president. By promoting science and technology among business and educational groups, Honeywell adds significantly to the region's economic potential and helps to structure community growth in a positive way.

Located on Albuquerque's West Mesa, Honeywell's new 100,000-square-foot plant produces thermostats and other electronic temperature-control devices.

HOLIDAY INN DE LAS CRUCES

Conveniently located near the junction of interstate highways 10 and 25, Holiday Inn de Las Cruces has become one of the most popular stopping places for travelers in southern New Mexico. Less than an hour's drive from El Paso and the Mexican frontier, Las Cruces has strong ties to the Hispanic culture that flourishes on both sides of the border. The inn's founder, C.W. "Buddy" Ritter, has a deep interest in the regional culture that is reflected in the architecture and decor of his establishment. In planning the Holiday Inn de Las Cruces Ritter has emphasized southwestern style and charm without foregoing the usual amenities.

After three years of preliminary planning Ritter engaged two leading designers, Frances Wood of Albuquerque and John Meigs from San Patricio, to ensure that his hotel projected an authentic atmosphere. Together they employed historical themes in decorating the lobby, dining rooms, and guest rooms using antique pictures and artifacts collected by Ritter through the years. Arriving guests pass through two massive Spanish colonial doors to enter a small patio embellished with Mexican tile. They are greeted by bellmen and desk clerks dressed in appropriate costumes. One cocktail lounge recalls the exploits of the controversial Mexican revolutionary Pancho Villa; another focuses on Billy the Kid, New Mexico's most famous gunslinger.

A native of Las Cruces, Ritter attended local schools and New Mexico Military Institute at Roswell. He also studied at Tulane University and graduated from New Mexico State University with a degree in banking and finance. After completing graduate work in hotel management at Michigan State and Cornell, he became the first certified hotel administrator in New Mexico. Before building his Holiday Inn, Ritter owned and managed the Lodge Hotel at Cloudcroft, a resort community high up in the Sacramento Mountains ninety miles northeast of Las Cruces. Ritter and his wife, the former Margaret Bonnell of Alamogordo, are the parents of three children.

In addition to the hotel, Ritter also owns and operates the Double Eagle Restaurant in La Mesilla, a historic community a mile west of Las Cruces. Despite the demands of his business interests, he has always found sufficient time for an active role in civic and trade associations. At various times he has served as an adviser on tourism to three New Mexico governors and is a past president of the New Mexico Amigos, a group of goodwill ambassadors. In 1970 Ritter was part of the United States delegation at the inauguration of Mexico's President Luis Echeverria. He now serves on the state's joint Border Commission with Mexico and is active in a wide variety of community organizations.

THE CITIZENS BANK OF CLOVIS

Incorporated on January 7, 1916, with capital stock of $25,000, The Citizens Bank of Clovis is the largest independent financial institution in east-central New Mexico. The bank's first president was George W. Singleton with S.A. Jones as cashier supervising daily operations; Charles E. Dennis followed as president, and then S.A. Jones. Clovis had become a trade center for the region's ranchers, farmers, and surrounding communities, and was a division point on the Santa Fe Railroad.

On February 19, 1920, a group headed by S.J. Boykin and A.W. Skarda organized Farmers State Bank of Clovis. Four years later The Citizens Bank and Farmers State merged, with Jones becoming president and Skarda becoming cashier. At the same time Jones and Skarda bought the assets of a bank that had gone into receivership in 1924. Properties acquired included the building at the northwest corner of Main and Grand streets, which served as The Citizens Bank headquarters until 1967.

Officers of The Citizens Bank made their mark in local business and political circles. S.A. Jones was state senator from Curry County from 1929 until his death in 1940. A.W. Skarda, Jones' successor as bank president, came to eastern New Mexico as a homesteader in 1906 where he started in banking as a bookkeeper. Skarda served as the Democratic National Committeeman from New Mexico from 1944 through 1952. He died on December 13, 1967, ending fifty-five years of banking.

T.E. Willmon, Jr., was born in Clovis, and went to work for The Citizens Bank on March 6, 1941. On March 29, 1966, after serving as a vice-president for many years, he became chief executive officer. He was appointed president of The Citizens Bank of Clovis on December 18, 1967, and still serves in that capacity. In addition to being acknowledged as one of New Mexico's outstanding bank presidents, he is well-versed in New Mexico history and lays claim to the title of New Mexico checker champion of 1947.

Since 1968 the bank's three directors have been Lynell G. Skarda, chairman of the board; Langdon L. Skarda, secretary of the board; and T.E. Willmon, Jr., president. Under their direction the bank, which moved to a handsome new building at Fifth and Pile streets in 1967, has increased its assets to more than $145 million.

The Citizens Bank of Clovis' circular building is one of the most unusual in the Southwest.

NAVAJO REFINING COMPANY

An aerial view from the early 1960s of the refinery's south plant. The building in the right foreground is the old Artesia Hotel, a popular gathering spot for oil men that was demolished in 1976.

In 1981 Navajo consolidated its offices in a new headquarters building. The "car cracker" tower in the background is no longer used but still serves as a local landmark.

One of New Mexico's major processors of petroleum products, Navajo Refining Company has its refinery and headquarters in the Pecos Valley on the eastern edge of Artesia. The first small refinery in Artesia was built in 1925 to provide an outlet for crude oil being produced in the new Artesia Field, which had been discovered the previous year. As the Artesia Field continued to grow, a second small refinery was put into operation in 1931 to handle the increased crude oil production. Drilling and production continued to increase at a rapid pace and by 1939 additional refining capacity was needed. Another small refinery, constructed during 1939-1940 by Joe Head, a Clovis oil man, was acquired in 1941 by a group of Fort Worth businessmen who enlarged the plant capacity to 1,800 barrels per day. Doing business as New Mexico Asphalt and Refining Company, this third refinery continued to expand over the years and by 1952 had reached a through capacity of 11,000 barrels per day. Over this same period the first two Artesia refineries underwent ownership changes, expansion of some processing facilities, and dismantling of old, obsolete facilities. Prominent names of refinery owners during this period were Continental Oil Company and Robert O. Anderson, a young entrepreneur from Chicago.

In 1953 the Texans sold the third refinery to Anderson, who by this time had acquired ten years' experience in the Artesia oil fields. Anderson subsequently became an industry legend by serving as president and chairman of the board of Atlantic Richfield Company, the giant energy and natural resources conglomerate now known as ARCO. After six years' management by Anderson, mighty Continental Oil Company acquired the refinery in 1959 under a twenty-year lease-purchase agreement.

Using interconnected pipelines, Continental joined the plant to an adjacent facility operated by the same company, making it the largest refinery in New Mexico. The combined operation manufactured gasoline, diesel, jet fuel, asphalt, and other products that were primarily marketed through a pipeline distribution network reaching from Artesia to El Paso, Tucson, Phoenix, and Albuquerque.

Federal regulatory agencies viewed Continental's expansion with disfavor, however. In 1961 the Justice Department filed an antitrust suit against the corporation, charging that the acquisition left several independent marketers without a source of supply. After lengthy litigation, the United States Supreme Court ordered Conoco to divest itself of the Artesia refinery. Acting in compliance, Continental sold the plant, pipelines, and terminals in 1969 to Navajo Refining Company, a newly formed group headed by C.L. Norsworthy, Jr., of Dallas, with Holly Corporation of Azusa, California, as general partner. Holly became sole owner of Navajo in 1975.

Since taking control in 1969, under the leadership of Fred G. Hansen and Jack P. Reid as presidents of Navajo and Lamar Norsworthy as chairman of Holly, Navajo has invested over sixty million dollars in plant expansion and related improvements. More than three million dollars has been spent on environmental-protection equipment to comply with state and federal regulations. In 1981 the company completed two major projects that included a major addition of refining equipment and completion of a new office complex. As a result of the refining process improvements, gasoline production capacity has increased to over 700,000 gallons per day. In fifteen years the staff has more than doubled to 320 employees with an annual payroll of over eleven million dollars. Each year Navajo pays approximately $380 million to several thousand crude-oil operators and royalty holders and makes extensive purchases from material suppliers and service contractors in the area. Contributions such as this make Navajo Refining Company a major contributor to the economic well-being of Artesia and southeastern New Mexico.

KOAT-TV

Part of the communications revolution that swept the nation after World War II, KOAT-TV went on the air September 23, 1953, as an affiliate of American Broadcasting Company. Albuquerque's second TV station, the new enterprise was operated by Alvarado Television, Inc., an organization headed by Albert M. Caldwell. The station's debut had been delayed by a licensing freeze imposed in 1950 by the Federal Communications Commission to unsnarl a nationwide scramble for frequencies. With government restrictions lifted, regular broadcasting began September 23 on Channel 7 following a few days of tests. Early favorites included "Abbott and Costello," "Cavalcade of America," "What's My Line?," and wrestling, live from Albuquerque's National Guard Armory. A local consumer loan company sponsored the first program of news, weather, and sports. ABC network programs were received on film with the exception of a few live Tello feeds such as Friday night boxing.

Like many other pioneers in television, KOAT grew out of a radio station with the same call letters established in 1947 by Rio Grande Broadcasting, Inc. For a few years both stations shared quarters at 122 Tulane Drive Southeast, near the University of New Mexico campus. Management soon sold off the radio division, which later became station KQEO. In 1956 Channel 7 greatly enlarged its broadcast area by moving all transmission facilities to the crest of the Sandia Mountains high above Albuquerque's east side. The antenna stands at 10,852 feet above sea level and is the nation's highest TV antenna. The following year KOAT was purchased by Clinton McKinnon, who also owned a television station in Tucson. While under McKinnon's control, the Albuquerque station began to receive ABC network programs by microwave from Phoenix. He also moved corporate offices to a new location on University Boulevard.

KOAT's early success attracted the attention of other outside investors. After enjoying a period of growth and expansion, McKinnon sold the station in 1963 to a group from Pennsylvania who retained ownership for six years. In May 1969 Channel 7 was purchased by the present owner, Pulitzer Broadcasting Co. of St. Louis. A far-flung conglomerate, the Pulitzer media group grew out of one of the nation's great newspapers, the St. Louis *Post Dispatch.* Local autonomy at KOAT has been maintained, however, through the leadership of Max Sklower, general manager since 1958, who has consistently maintained a policy of community concern and involvement.

Presently Channel 7's broadcast area covers some 160,000 square miles in four states through an extensive translator network. During the past five years KOAT has ranked among the top five ABC affiliates in the United States in terms of viewing audience. Since its beginning, job opportunities have increased from a handful of employees in 1953 to a staff of 140. In 1980 KOAT moved into new headquarters, a handsome building of advanced architectural design at the corner of Comanche and Carlisle in northeast Albuquerque.

KOAT-TV's studio facilities, constructed in 1980, are among the most technologically advanced in the Southwest.

PATRONS

The following individuals, companies, and organizations have made a valuable commitment to the quality of this publication. Windsor Publications and the Historical Society of New Mexico gratefully acknowledge their participation in *New Mexico: The Distant Land.*

Adobe Gallery
Artservices of Santa Fe
Atkinson Trading Company*
Barker Realty, Inc.*
Big Jo Lumber Company*
Blake's Lotaburger, Inc.*
Bowlin's Incorporated
Bruce Caird Realty
Celsius Energy Company - Southern Exploration Division
The Citizens Bank of Clovis*
College of Santa Fe*
Wayne A. Delamater, M.D., P.A.
Joe D. Dennis
Mr. and Mrs. Richard Donnelly
D.W. Eakin Company
Elliott Enterprises, Inc.
La Placita Dining Rooms*
Gas Company of New Mexico*
Greater Albuquerque Chamber of Commerce*
Mrs. Frank S. Griswold
Brad L. Hays
Holiday Inn de Las Cruces*
Honeywell, Inc.*
Hooten/Stahl Inc. Realtors*
Host International
John and Mary House
Arlen Janke
Phil Kendall
KOAT-TV*
Koogle and Pouls Engineering, Inc.*
W.C. Kruger and Associates, Architects & Planners, Inc.*
La Fonda*
Emily and Bob Lovell
The General D.L. McBride Museum
The Honorable Lord Manning
Navajo Refining Company*
The New Mexican*
New Mexico Blue Cross and Blue Shield, Inc.*
New Mexico Federal Savings and Loan Association*
The Peters Corporation*
Pfaltzgraff-Robinson, P.C.
Public Service Company of New Mexico*
Rancho Encantado*
The Regent of Albuquerque*
Senator Tom Rutherford
St. John's College*
Mr. and Mrs. Dave Sorenson
Sperry Corporation*
Tinnin Enterprises*
The Toles Company
United New Mexico*
Valliant Company*
Wadle Galleries Ltd.
Warren, Inc.
Woods Insurance Service

*Partners in Progress of *New Mexico: The Distant Land.* The histories of these companies and organizations appear in Chapter VIII, beginning on page 141.

Although service was frequently uncomfortable and unreliable, stagecoaches provided an important means of transportation in nineteenth-century New Mexico. Standing before the Meredith and Ailman Bank in Silver City, driver and passengers posed for this photo prior to their departure for Georgetown, New Mexico, circa 1885. MNM (#11933)

ACKNOWLEDGMENTS

I have incurred many debts while assembling the photographs reproduced in this volume. Although it is impossible to thank everyone who rendered assistance, I am particularly grateful to the following: Michael Miller, Christine Roybal, Louellen Martinez, and Kay Dorman of the New Mexico State Records Center and Archives; Arthur Olivas, Richard Rudisill, and Sue Critchfield of the Museum of New Mexico; Jan Barnhart of Special Collections, University of New Mexico General Library; and Fred Mang, Jr., of the Southwestern Regional Headquarters, National Park Service. All have been generous with time and welcome advice.

John O. Baxter
Santa Fe
February 1985

The New Mexico Historical Society is the memory of New Mexico. The Society has long shown that it is dedicated not only to assembling and preserving knowledge of the heritage we share, but in making it available to all comers. I am just a storyteller, and everyone knows that a storyteller without a memory is not worth much. We all are grateful to the society; I am just the one to be saying it here.

John Conron of the society especially deserves thanks for seeing this project through. We were neighbors when I first came to Santa Fe and ended up carpentering to pay the bills. John hired me—it seems a long time ago. Thanks, John, for that and this.

I owe special thanks to Dr. Myra Ellen Jenkins, former director of the New Mexico State Archives, for keeping me on track. Storytellers can play only where historians have labored. Actually, sometimes Myra Ellen almost frightens me, though respect is becoming tempered with affection. (Stern phone call: "It's the *Ordinances* of 1573, Dan, not the *Laws* of 1573!") If any error like that one slipped into this book, it must be that I put it in after she saw it. I am very thankful to her, and to David Brugge and Spenser Wilson, for critically reading the manuscript.

There are two other historians, not specifically connected with this manuscript but who have taught me much about New Mexico, to whom I owe much: Drs. Marc Simmons and John Kessell. Some of my best history lessons have been while walking the road to Chimayo with John, or stacking firewood with Marc. Gentlemen, I thank you. Now Marc, get back to your biography of Kit Carson, and John, resume your great study of Vargas. We need your work!

Finally, to Laurel Paley at Windsor Publications: Laurel, this is the first time I've been totally unbending, but I know that you are editing this, and I demand that you leave in this appreciation for your invaluable work on the project, and your putting up with my deficiencies. Thank you.

I've promised the people involved with this a Dutch Oven supper when finally it's done. It's time to go heat the ovens.

Dan Murphy
Santa Fe
February 1985

SUGGESTION FOR FURTHER READING

New Mexico is a fascinating state, and every day a scholar somewhere is digging into yet another corner of its history. Any good library has publications with the details unearthed: Marc Simmons on Spanish Colonial ironwork or early witchcraft; Al Schroeder on the history of the Apaches; France Scholes on the seventeenth century; Polly Schaafsma on rock art; Paige Christiansen on mining; Stuart Northrop on fossils; Erna Fergusson on anything; the list goes on and on and will be longer tomorrow. But there are a few books that are bedrock. Some are old, some are not, but they are good places to begin to read about this very special place. Here are a few of my favorites, with a blanket apology for the many left out.

Ross Calvin, *Sky Determines,* University of New Mexico Press, 1965. The book ties the events of the state to its climate, landforms, and natural history, and is a good antidote to histories which deal only with humans interacting with humans.

David Lavender, *The Southwest,* University of New Mexico Press, 1984. Many of us waited anxiously while this skilled researcher and writer worked on this book. (His *Bent's Old Fort* already had captivated us.) Worth the wait, the book places New Mexico in the broad context of the Southwest.

John Kessell, *Kiva, Cross, and Crown,* Government Printing Office Press, no date. The best thing the Government Printing Office ever did, the book is the story of Pecos Pueblo and the mission established there, which serves as the focus for a much broader history. Fine writing and scholarship characterize this volume, and, unexpectedly for GPO, it is well designed with wonderful illustrations. When each new character appears, so does his florid signature, copied from a document. This is my favorite book for sitting by a fire, reading slowly.

Herbert Eugene Bolton, *Coronado: Knight of Pueblos and Plains,* University of New Mexico Press, 1964. This is the "old reliable" we all had in college and an exciting rediscovery for me twenty years later. If you've not read it lately, get it out again. Bolton is always good for demolishing the silly idea that there wasn't much here before the Anglos (including me) came.

John Nichols, *The Milagro Beanfield War,* Random House, 1974. I debated whether to put in this hilarious novel, but it may be the best (and most enjoyable) way to understand a small New Mexican village. I have five friends who assure me they know exactly which village he used for a model—and each insists on a different village. This means Nichols has grasped something essential.

Paul Horgan, *Lamy of Santa Fe, The Centuries of Santa Fe,* and of course his masterpiece, *Great River.* Some people have made a career of trying to find mistakes in the latter, but no mind: you can't miss with a great writer and a vast subject.

Robert and Florence Lister, *Those Who Came Before,* Southwest Parks and Monuments Association, Tucson. Well illustrated, this is the best overview of the state's archeological story. Dr. Lister was the chief archeologist of the National Park Service and director of the Chaco Project.

Bernard DeVoto, *The Year of Decision: 1846,* deals with New Mexico via the Kearny Expedition only, but is still a treasure for its writing. No objectivity here: DeVoto flaunts his opinions, but in prose so absorbing that you don't mind. You can actually do the old trick of putting your finger anywhere and finding a superlative sentence.

I hate to stop, but it is time to go read a book, and one not listed here. You will have to find it for yourself.

INDEX

This book was set in
Helvetica, Times Roman, and
Times Roman Italic typefaces.

It was printed on
70-Pound Acid-Free
Mead Offset Enamel paper
and bound by
Walsworth Publishing Company.

ONZALES
DELMONI
Rud. Cronau 83